OWN YOUR FUTURE

OWN YOUR FUTURE

HOW TO THINK LIKE AN ENTREPRENEUR AND THRIVE IN AN UNPREDICTABLE ECONOMY

PAUL B. BROWN

WITH CHARLES F. KIEFER AND
LEONARD A. SCHLESINGER

AMACOM

AMERICAN MANAGEMENT ASSOCIATION
New York • Atlanta • Brussels • Chicago • Mexico City •
San Francisco • Shanghai • Tokyo • Toronto • Washington, D.C.

Bulk discounts available. For details visit:
www.amacombooks.org/go/specialsales
Or contact special sales:
Phone: 800-250-5308
Email: specialsls@amanet.org
View all the AMACOM titles at: www.amacombooks.org
American Management Association: www.amanet.org

Library of Congress Cataloging-in-Publication Data
Brown, Paul B.
   Own your future : how to think like an entrepreneur and thrive in an unpredictable economy / Paul B. Brown ; with Charles F. Kiefer and Leonard A. Schlesinger.
      pages cm
   Includes index.
   ISBN-13: 978-0-8144-3409-3 (hardcover)
   ISBN-10: 0-8144-3409-6 (hardcover)
   ISBN-13: 978-0-8144-3410-9 (ebook)
   1. Success in business. 2. Entrepreneurship. 3. Career development.
4. Success. I. Kiefer, Charles F. II. Schlesinger, Leonard A. III. Title.
   HF5386.B8763 2014
   658.4'09—dc23   2014005052

About AMA
American Management Association (www.amanet.org) is a world leader in talent development, advancing the skills of individuals to drive business success. Our mission is to support the goals of individuals and organizations through a complete range of products and services, including classroom and virtual seminars, webcasts, webinars, podcasts, conferences, corporate and government solutions, business books, and research. AMA's approach to improving performance combines experiential learning—learning through doing—with opportunities for ongoing professional growth at every step of one's career journey.

Printing number
10 9 8 7 6 5 4 3 2 1

CONTENTS

PREFACE

The world doesn't need another book about entrepreneurs. The world does, however, need a book on how to navigate the
complexity, uncertainty, and risks of modern work life—and that is
what you will find here.

As you will read, we hold up the experiences of serial entrepreneurs—those individuals who have created at least two successful
ventures—as role models. Why? Because there is nothing more
uncertain than starting a business, and serial entrepreneurs are
masters at it.

The question motivating us as we set out to write this book was
straightforward: How can those of us who don't necessarily want to
start businesses of our own apply what serial entrepreneurs have
learned about navigating uncertainty in order to increase the odds for
success in our personal and professional lives?

Like many people, you may never have thought of yourself as an
entrepreneur, or even that entrepreneurship has any relationship to

your life. But the capacity to think and act entrepreneurially has increasingly become a critical life skill—vital in a world where the levels of uncertainty are high and the challenges that uncertainty causes are daunting.

What serial entrepreneurs have in common is making uncertainty work to their advantage. As you will see, what works for them will work for you as well, and it isn't as hard as you think. You actually knew what to do when you were an infant, and you unlearned it when you went through an education process that is entirely rooted in how to manage our lives in a predictable world. In the pages ahead, we will help you rediscover how you can regain the core skills of thinking and acting entrepreneurially.

SMALL, SMART STEPS

Central to this book are the benefits of smart action. Decades of research—most notably by Saras Sarasvathy of the University of Virginia's Darden School of Business—and everyday observation show that the best entrepreneurs don't overthink and worry about all possible outcomes. They consciously and deliberately take small, smart steps toward their goal.

We'll summarize for you how they do this, and reveal how they evaluate what they learn from taking those small, smart steps, and how what they learn shapes what they do next.

As you will see, we looked at how entrepreneurs actually behave—rejecting the myths and misconceptions about the lives of entrepreneur superstars. Instead, we drew upon the entrepreneurial life experiences of all kinds of people (not just entrepreneurs) and the array of tools and approaches they employed to succeed, so that we all can learn from these experiences as well.

So, think of this book as an owner's manual for having a more successful life. We're not all going to become entrepreneurs as traditionally defined, but we must all still think and act the way they do. In today's uncertain world, this is the surest path to achieving what we want—in work and all aspects of our lives.

Like most things in life, our thinking about all this is a work in progress. You can follow how it evolves at the blog Paul writes for *Forbes*: *Action Trumps Everything*, http://www.forbes.com/sites/actiontrumpseverything/.

OWN YOUR FUTURE

INTRODUCTION

"We Love the Idea. It's Just Too Darn Depressing to Publish."

If you hit me over the head long enough, the message will finally get through.

That, in fifteen words, sums up the long, roundabout trip I took in order to bring this book into being.

But it was well worth the journey. Let me explain.

A couple of years ago Len Schlesinger, Charlie Kiefer, and I wrote a book called *Just Start: Take Action, Embrace Uncertainty, Create the Future*. We addressed what organizations and people should do when they don't know what to do, and laid out a course of action to follow when you or your organization are faced with uncertainty.

Today, one of the most uncertain things imaginable is trying to predict whether you're going to have a job in five years. So, that's our focus this time around. Specifically, we set off to answer this question: *How can you create a prosperous career in an economic world that is being radically reshaped in real time?*

It turns out to be an extremely important question because it looks to us like there are only three types of people who can depend on continuing employment. They are:

1. **Skilled tradesmen.** For people working in a skilled trade, like plumbers and electricians, the only concern, other than the overall health of the economy—which, of course, is no small thing—is the increasing trend toward using plug-in parts. (When customers can do the work themselves—quickly, safely, and for less cost—there is little reason to hire you.)

2. **People who can live with how their profession is evolving.** There is always going to be a demand for nurses and teachers, for example. And if you can accept the trends—heavier workloads and more online (as opposed to face-to-face) interactions—then you can continue as you are. You might grow progressively unhappy in the job ("This is not why I signed up to be a nurse"; "I hate teaching to the test"), but if you are good, you will have a job in a field that will sort of, kind of resemble the one you entered.

3. **People who can coast safely into the sunset.** This scenario used to be far more prevalent than it is today. There were employees who would, in essence, retire in place five or even sometimes ten years before their official retirement age. Today, some companies are still nice enough to allow long-time valued employees to coast, but it is likely going to be for five or ten *months* (and it is far from being a guarantee).

But these are the only exceptions we found. If you work in an industry that is in total flux (publishing or music) or starting to unravel (finance), or one that you suspect might soon change radically—or, if your career has recently been upended (or soon might be) or has never really gotten going, or you feel stuck and frustrated—your job is probably going away.

But it doesn't have to be that depressing.

THE GOOD NEWS . . .

Talking to people who are coping successfully with all this turmoil—and reading the research being done, especially the work of Saras Sarasvathy, who teaches at the Darden School of Business at the University of Virginia—turned up some extremely good news. There is a way to deal with all this upheaval and come out in a potentially much better place than you are today. The solution is to act the way successful entrepreneurs do. Not by necessarily starting your own company—although as we will discuss, that is certainly an option—but by approaching your career the way successful entrepreneurs handle the unknown.

When people write about entrepreneurs, they invariably focus on their behavior: What did Howard Schultz or Michael Dell or Martha Stewart do to build their companies? If you take that approach, you probably would conclude that every entrepreneur is unique, and so there is little to be learned from studying them; that is, you would have to be Howard Schultz to start Starbucks, Michael Dell to create Dell, and Martha Stewart to begin the company she did.

And, you'd be right.

But—and it is a huge but—if instead of looking at their behavior, you look at how the most successful entrepreneurs *think*, you will find amazing similarities in how they reason, approach obstacles, and take advantage of opportunities. And it's from examining that pattern that we can all benefit, because it will give us a set of tools we can use to deal with the increasing amount of uncertainty we face.

Here's the path they usually take.

1. **What they set out to do is what they want to do.** While passion was not absolutely required, before they started they had

real, honest-to-goodness desire. In other words, as they got their business underway, the feeling was substantially more than "it seems like a good idea."

2. **They quickly take a *small* step toward their goal** . . . using whatever means they have at hand. They don't want to over-commit or move so far so fast that they can't recover. Equally important, they don't spend a lot of time asking "what if" or thinking about what *might* happen. They take a small step toward what they desire and find out.

3. **After taking that small step, they stop to see what they have learned.** Maybe they learn that their initial goal is still a good one. Maybe the market is telling them that they need to go in another direction. Maybe they discover that they don't have the desire anymore. Maybe, after considering what they have learned after taking that first small step, they realize there is something else they would much rather do. The point is, they always pause and reflect after each step they take toward their goal.

4. **Once they understand what they've learned, they take another small step** . . . and go through the cycle again.

In other words, the formula for success (if there is one) is figuring out what you truly want to do. Then, once you know: **Act. Learn.** Then **Build** (off of what you find). And then **Repeat** (the process).

> There is a proven path for dealing with
> uncertainty: Proceed as proven entrepreneurs do.
> After all, there is nothing more uncertain than
> starting a business, and these people have done
> it successfully. What has worked for them
> will work for you.

This ALBR* process continues until you are happy with the result, or you decide that you don't want to (or can't afford to) go on.

The way that entrepreneurs approach uncertainty is a plausible—and perhaps even perfect—way of preparing for an uncertain economic future. It is a more practical replacement for the traditional career planning that we all know.

We'll explore this idea in detail in Chapter 2, but let's just touch on it here. You know how traditional career planning works: You imagine what job you want to have at a fixed point in the future—say, five years from now—and then work backward from there, figuring out what you have to do to get from where you are now to where you want to be. What classes you need to take, for instance, and what job assignments, and the like.

The problem with this approach is that it does you absolutely no good if your industry goes away. Let's say you were an assistant store manager at Blockbuster who was planning on being a regional man-

---

* In *Just Start* (Harvard Business Press, 2012), my coauthors Len Schlesinger and Charlie Kiefer refer to this process as simply ALB. They believe the repeat part is implicit. Since I am the kind of person who needs to be beaten over the head to have an idea sink in, I am going to use the R to make repeating an integral—and explicit—part of the process.

ager in five years. When the industry was stable you would carve out a path that probably looked like this: You would become an associate store manager in year one, store manager in year three, and regional manager (in charge of a bunch of stores) in year five. But all that planning goes for naught if your video chain—and all the others—go under. In an environment where that is likely to happen, traditional career planning is useless.

So, how should that Blockbuster employee, let's call her Kayla, determine what she should do next? Here's what she would do if she followed the ALBR model.

She'd start by figuring out what she wants to do.

Well, she started working at Blockbuster because she truly loves movies and introducing people to some of her favorites (and learning from them about gems she might have missed). Where else could she do that? She took a number of small steps to find out.

Step 1. She approached a couple of the big cinema chains but quickly learned her primary job there would be to push as many high-margin soft drinks and snacks as possible. Movies would be an afterthought, and the decision about what to show was always made at corporate. Working in a theater, she would have no input on what was shown. That wasn't what she wanted to do. And so on to the next small step.

Step 2. The independent/foreign movie theaters were too snooty for her taste. Kayla believes movies are to be shared and celebrated. Your opinion of them, she argues, should not be used to belittle someone who wouldn't know a pan wipe—a shot where a stationary camera turns horizontally, revealing a new scene—from a pan of chicken. Another dead end.

Step 3. She talked to people who ran various film studies departments and those who had earned an MFA (master of fine arts degree), and while the idea of receiving credit for watching movies was appealing, she really didn't see what she would be able to do with the degree that she couldn't do now. So, that wasn't an option, either.

In each of these cases there was neither a huge investment of time or resources in trying to determine what career path to follow. Instead of spending hours and hours researching, planning, and searching who, exactly, to mail her résumé to, Kayla simply called around and talked to friends of friends. She took small steps and learned from each one. The learning in these cases was negative, in the sense that she learned she didn't love any of the ideas she came up with—although knowing what you don't want to do can be extremely valuable.

However, in the course of all her small steps, she met Peter, a recent MBA, who was convinced that there was a market for a revival house in town. It would be the sort of place that could show the great old movies on a huge screen. He had worked out the numbers—and it definitely looked like you could turn a profit—and found the perfect location. But after saying he really loved *Casablanca, Citizen Kane, Stagecoach,* and *Unforgiven,* Peter hadn't a clue about what kind of movies to show.

When last we checked, Kayla and Peter have joined forces, and we have to admit their preliminary programming decisions—Femme Fatale Fridays and Weird Wednesdays—sound appealing. They expect to have their grand opening, complete with klieg lights firing into the sky and a red carpet for local "celebrities" like the mayor, soon.

Kayla's story is a good one. But how do we know that the Act.

Learn. Build. Repeat. model is the right path for dealing with all the economic uncertainty we face?

Well, of course, we can't know for sure. We are dealing with the unknown (i.e., what is going to happen in the global marketplace), so there are no guarantees. But, the approach certainly resonates.

Convinced that I was onto something, I came up with a title that I loved: "Thriving in the Pink Slip Economy." I started talking to my friends, some of whom are book editors, and everyone said it was an extremely big idea and would make a terrific book. I was thrilled. And then they said something that got me hopelessly depressed.

"But it's too much of a downer. Nobody is going to spend $22 for a book like that."

"What do you mean?" I asked.

"Well, for one thing, you are telling people that we have entered a period of permanent downsizing, so they are going to face a constant threat of being fired. Who wants to hear they are going to spend their working life in a pink slip economy and that they could lose their job at any moment? And for another, you are saying they are going to need a new set of skills. Obtaining them sounds hard, especially for people who don't have an entrepreneurial bone in their body. No one is going to buy a depressing career book."

In response, I tried to argue that the economy has entered a period of upheaval that shows no sign of abating, and that even if you couldn't sell your mother a box of Girl Scout cookies, I would be able to show you a way to think and act more entrepreneurially.

But I couldn't change their minds.

And then I realized I was going about my argument all wrong. Instead of saying "You're doomed. You are going to be thrown out of work. You better understand that you have to get your head out of the sand and prepare for a radically new future," there was a far better way of getting the point across.

Yes, of course, the economic world is changing. But that change can be a good thing. It gives us all a chance to rethink what it is we truly want to do with our lives. Given how busy we all are, we often don't get the chance to do that.

SO IS THIS A CAREER BOOK?

Were well-meaning friends right when they referred to this as a career book?

Sort of. Calling this a "career" book is analogous to saying it sometimes rains in Seattle or London. It is certainly true, but it is understating things just a bit.

Yes, by all means, this book offers a (unique) way to maneuver through all the upheaval in the workplace. But the purpose here is far broader. Think of it as a career guide for people who don't buy career guides. We believe it can be helpful for people who:

1. Are looking for a job—whether for the first time or when reentering the workforce (e.g., after a stint in the service, being out on disability, staying at home for a while to be a parent, or after losing their job)

2. Want to advance (faster) in their careers

3. Feel stuck

4. Believe, with good reason, that their industry/career/ position is in jeopardy

5. Want to be prepared for the worst

6. Simply want to keep their options open

Perhaps, most of all, this guide is for people in denial, or those who wrongly believe that the upheaval that has affected just about every industry you can think of won't affect their industry, their organization—and them.

And if you can start thinking about these issues while you still have a job, you will be substantially ahead of the game.

That is a far more uplifting approach to the topic, and it more accurately reflects what we wanted to write. We know it is still going to be difficult to convince everyone that their jobs are at risk. The natural inclination is to deny it and say, "Sure, scores of industries have been upended, but mine is safe. And even if it isn't, I'll be okay (because of my unique circumstances or skills)."

Odds are that isn't going to be the case, and you will see why.

But the more appealing part of the book, I promise, is that you'll understand how you can take advantage of all the economic upheaval to end up with a job or career that is perhaps more satisfying than the one you have or envision right now.

And should you and your industry manage not to be affected by all the radical change around us, the new skills you learn will stand you in good stead going forward at your current job.

Armed with this much more positive message, I tested the

market. With the help of Charlie Kiefer and Len Schlesinger, I wrote a series of blogs for the *Harvard Business Review*, and the response was extremely encouraging. So we plunged into the book wholeheartedly, and the results are what you hold in your hand.

We promise it will be worth your time. Enjoy.

SECTION I

Did the Earth Move?
Yes. It Did.

CHAPTER 1

Why Everyone Will Have to Become an Entrepreneur

Here is our basic argument: You can benefit from what the people who are the best at navigating uncertainty already know.

Everyone? *Everyone* must become an entrepreneur?

You are right to be skeptical, if you define *entrepreneur* as someone who creates a for-profit business. But that is a very limited definition. It doesn't include people who start things for social reasons. Or community reasons. And it certainly doesn't include people in organizations who take an entrepreneurial approach to solving the challenges they (and the enterprises that employ them) face.

So maybe a more accurate title for this chapter would have been "Why everyone will need to master entrepreneurial thought and action to thrive in the increasingly uncertain world in which we live." Or maybe even "This-is-a-book-for-people-who-never-plan-on-ever-becoming-an-entrepreneur-but-need-to-pay-attention-anyway-because-the-universe-does-not-always-behave-the-way-they-want-it-to-and-you-may-just-end-up-needing-new-skills."

But while those titles might be more precise, they struck our publisher as "clunky." And so we are stuck with a chapter title that may not be completely accurate . . . but the underlying premise certainly is. While everyone doesn't need to go out and start a business tomorrow, it's certain that we all need to know when it is appropriate to think and act entrepreneurially today.

You don't need to do much more than read the daily paper or look around to see what is happening to your friends and neighbors to understand why this is true. Given the steady improvements in technology that are automating people out of jobs, corporations are reluctant to hire new employees. With constant headcount reductions (designed to boost profits) and the outsourcing of jobs, it is just silly to expect that you are going to join a company today and be set for life. (The fact that this statement strikes you as obvious, and that no one under the age of 40 knows what the phrase "company man" means, shows you just how far the workplace has changed since the first Baby Boomers entered it.)

> The market doesn't care about your industry, your company, or you. Your career will probably be disrupted. More than once. This is just (an unfortunate) fact. You need to be ready.

The point? We'd better be prepared to create something (on the side, at the very least) no matter what we are currently doing for a living. That's true whether you are age 18 or 58. Even if you work for the world's best company today, someone could acquire the firm tomorrow, or a new invention could render your entire industry obsolete. (Rent many movies from a freestanding video store lately? Bought any maps or a new set of encyclopedias?) Your work life is not completely within your control.

And obviously, if you are out of work, you may be forced to become an entrepreneur. In any case, you will want to add entrepreneurial skills to your job-hunting repertoire.

But even if you are not one of the people who are affected by all the change sweeping through the economy, if you keep doing things as you are in your current job, chances are you will fall behind coworkers who show more initiative, creativity, and entrepreneurial spirit.

You might smugly think "never in this company" or "my union/boss/seniority will protect me." You'd be wrong. Companies need and will reward people who take an entrepreneurial approach.

Ah, some of you say, but I am late in life and I can coast to the finish. This may be true, and it points to the one exception to our assertion that everyone will need to employ entrepreneurial thought and action at some point in their lives.

If, in fact, you are independently wealthy (either because you have a lot of money or a secure retirement package) *and* you no longer care to be productive, then you probably won't need to be entrepreneurial.

But let's say you don't *have* to work. What will you do? Maybe you can find a great job, but most companies don't like hiring old coots or people who don't really need the gig. And you will be taking that job away from someone who does need it, perhaps desperately. Nope, no one is going to hand you your "second act." You are going to have to start your own thing.

The only people we can think of who won't need to be entrepreneurial are those who can—and want to—coast safely to the finish line of life while playing only with their families and friends. Of course, whether you can coast carries some risk. Nothing these days is all that certain. Ask the people who invested their retirement savings with

Bernie Madoff, or the state workers who are getting their pensions cut, or all those healthy older people who are in very real risk of outliving their money. It wouldn't hurt for you to activate your entrepreneurial abilities, just in case! And it could be fun.

IT'S LESS COMPLICATED THAN YOU MIGHT THINK

In fact, it's relatively easy to become entrepreneurial. It simply involves remembering and employing a style of thinking and acting that you've probably been neglecting since you were a child. We are going to show you how to use it once again. And as you will see, each step you take toward reactivating this long-forgotten skill will build your competence and confidence. It will enable you to generate new opportunities and new alternatives that were previously inconceivable.

So, what specifically will you learn from this book? Well, we are going to begin, in Section I, by reminding you—quickly—just how much has changed when it comes to finding and keeping a job. (When we are in the eye of a hurricane, as most of us are in while doing our day-to-day jobs, it is hard to see and understand everything that is swirling around us.) By the time we're done, you will know why the old corporate world is never coming back, and you'll understand why, as a result, you will need to change your approach to employment.

In Section II, we explain the new model that has worked well for many people as they try to cope with all the changes we're going through. We sum it up this way: Act. Learn. Build. Repeat. It's exactly the same approach that serial entrepreneurs, people who have started two or more successful companies, usually follow.

Why look to them? That's simple. When it comes to the world of work today, most things are uncertain. And there is nothing more uncertain than starting a business, and these people are masters at it. That's why in navigating your future, you want to take the same approach they do every time they journey into the unknown.

That means you need to:

➤ Determine your desire.

➤ Take a small step toward it.

➤ Learn from taking that small step.

➤ Build off that learning and take another step.

➤ Learn from that next step . . . and so on.

In other words, Act. Learn. Build. Repeat. We will show you exactly how this approach works—and could work for you.

Once you are armed with an approach that will allow you to deal with uncertainty, the question is: Where do you want to go? We deal with that in Section III, where we also give examples of people who answered that question by deciding to become entrepreneurs themselves.

But, of course, you may choose not to trundle off immediately and start your own firm. Section IV provides examples of how the Act. Learn. Build. Repeat. model can be used in other ways, such as finding a new job and entering the workforce. And in the appendixes, we will explore how it can also be used in schools, in nonprofits, and to make our communities better.

Here's the takeaway: The world of work has changed dramatically. Let's see how you can thrive within this brave new world.

WHAT WE JUST COVERED— *AND WHAT'S AHEAD*

1. Given the rapid and continuing change within the economy, job security withers by the day.

2. Increasingly, the only person you can rely on is you.

3. Knowing how to reason as the most successful entrepreneurs do will increase your chances for success.

We explain why these skills are so necessary in Chapter 2.

CHAPTER 2

What Happened?

You're worried. Frustrated. Confused. Or you can't seem to gain traction.

Or maybe you are in the middle of your career, and things are going well, but you don't like all the articles in the business press about how your entire industry could be in trouble. You are thinking you should do something before it's too late . . . but you aren't exactly sure what.

Or perhaps you are part of an industry that is (or has) imploded.

In these cases, and countless more you could think of that involve how work is now in flux, it's not your fault. The world has changed. That fact is sad and more than a little bit scary. But there is no doubting that it is true. The way we earn our living is in the process of changing forever. Here we are going to talk—briefly—about why, and then—in depth—about what you can do, not only to cope, but thrive.

We know the approach we are about to describe is successful because it is based on a proven method that has helped hundreds of thousands of people. What has worked for them will work for you.

Been to a music store lately? Drop off any photos to be processed? Used a pay phone? Read an afternoon newspaper (or been able to find a local morning one if you live in a small or even midsize city like New Orleans)? Bought a printed map? Placed a call from your hotel room—through the hotel's phone system? Used a travel agent to book a routine vacation?

Probably not.

And the trend of entire industries disappearing is only accelerating. Desktop computers are endangered; so are land (phone) lines and manufactured (mobile) housing, due to the glut of foreclosures on traditional homes. Faxes are now as quaint as dial-up Internet connections or rotary phones.

The list goes on and on and seems to grow longer by the day.

In fact, it's probably easier to name the tiny handful of professions and industries that will remain unchanged in the next twenty years than it is to write down the ones that will be altered—radically. All this upheaval is likely to throw you—and anyone else who is not prepared—out of a job.

When some people hear that, they say we are being hyperbolic. Or "sure, it happened in the industries you listed, but it won't happen in mine." Sticking your head in the sand is not the greatest strategy for preparing for the future. Hoping all this turmoil will pass you by is not a strategy.

But most people are not closing their eyes to what is going on. They are aware. But they simply don't know what to do. Ten years ago, if you lost your job at Kodak or Polaroid—or thought you soon would—you'd head over to some place like Fuji Film. However, when entire industries, like photofinishing, virtually disappear, that's no longer an option—and for those of us who are worried, we just don't know what a new alternative is. Like a deer caught in the headlights, we are frozen in place when it comes to thinking about how radically our professions could and most definitely will change, and what will happen to us as a result.

Sure, we know the one currency we all need to accumulate is knowledge. But by some accounts knowledge *is doubling* every five years—or faster—which explains why all these traditional industries and businesses are being replaced by new ones. As a consequence of this information explosion—and there is no other word for it—what you know rapidly becomes obsolete.

What's a person to do to survive, let alone thrive, in this environment?

DOES THIS SOUND FAMILIAR?

We didn't have a "typical reader" in mind when we began to write the book, but our guess is that Lynda Schwartz—who we discovered in the course of our research—is representative.

Schwartz, now in her late forties, had been a partner at one of the major accounting firms for thirteen years when she started to wonder if that was how she really wanted to spend the rest of her working life. "I did a spreadsheet to see what the benefits were to staying with the firm, and they became quite substantial if you stuck it out to age 50," she says, "but I found myself constantly referring to that spreadsheet as I went about my days. By the time I was 47, I realized three more years was a very long time."

Ultimately, she left the big firm and started her own consulting practice. "It was very liberating," she says. It allowed her the time to spend with her children who were adjusting to middle school, to assist a father-in-law struggling with Alzheimer's, and to work with the nonprofit she cared deeply about, while remaining engaged with her clients.

But that still left the challenge of how to shape her consulting practice going forward, or whether to shift to other kinds of work. She wanted to regain the sense of drive and purpose that had characterized her earlier career. When we spoke, this was the issue she was grappling with.

That question is unsettling, scary, and frustrating, because it is something we never anticipated when we finished school. Most of us prepared hard for the future we expected, and yet when it comes to our work life today things aren't turning out as we had planned. That's true if you have been laid off or are a recent college graduate who is underemployed; a manager who feels that he is stuck in his current position; or a member of the C-Suite who has the (probably justified) feeling that her company (and perhaps entire field) may implode around her.

This is *not* how we were told it was going to be.

Growing up we were led to believe that the future was predictable enough and if we studied hard we could obtain the work we wanted in a field we understood, and we would live happy and successful lives. It hasn't exactly worked out that way (even for those of us who are happy).

Why the disconnect between what we thought would happen and what is actually going on? We think the reason is pretty simple. The way we were taught to think and act works well when the future is predictable, but not so much in the world as it is now.

You know the steps for dealing with a predictable universe:

1. You (or your parents, teachers, or bosses) forecast what the future will be like and how you can have a successful life in it.

2. You construct a number of plans for achieving that life, picking the optimal one: that is, the one best suited to your abilities that will get you there in the shortest time, or with the least amount of effort, or that will produce the most pleasant journey.

3. You assemble whatever resources (education, money, etc.) are necessary to achieve your plan.

4. And then you go out and implement it.

We have become so indoctrinated with this way of thinking by our schools (with the way they taught us to think) and our organizations (with the way they go about solving problems) that "predict, plan, and implement" is more or less the only way we approach anything.

But what if a very smart approach to a knowable or predictable future is not smart at all when things can't be predicted—like now. And that fact is at the heart of the frustrations—and fear—most of us feel. Things simply aren't as predictable as they once were when it comes to plotting out a superior (and satisfying) career.

It's pretty scary when you can't plan and control your way to security, let alone the job you want.

In a world where you can no longer plan your way to success, what is the best way to achieve lifelong security and accomplish the things you care about? Answering that question—and, more important, giving you a detailed strategy and extremely specific tactics to follow, complete with lots of how-tos—is what this book is all about.

It was actually born out of frustration that, for us, took two forms.

First, your authors are personally living through everything we are discussing. Just because you are writing a book doesn't mean you live in a bubble. We have felt—and in some cases, have been victims of—all the disruptions whirling around all of us, and where it makes sense we will be using our own lives as part of the many case studies and examples that we'll share.

IT'S NOT JUST BUSINESS

We said in the introduction that this book is personal to us. And it is. Obviously, it is important to us. The three of us have reached the point in our lives where we try to work only on things that we believe are extremely worthwhile.

But it is also personal in the sense that we employ the principles we will be describing. Charlie has come by these lessons naturally. In the course of creating three separate companies, he has almost instinctively done what we will be advocating, as he has worked to unlock the latent potential in organizations of all kinds.

Len has advised hundreds of companies about how to best employ our ideas, and also has applied everything that we will be advocating in his personal and professional life, whether it was in business (as chief operating officer of Au Bon Pain and later Limited Brands) or academia (as a tenured professor at Harvard Business School or president of Babson College, which has been ranked the number-one school of entrepreneurship ever since people began creating the rankings).

Paul, who is now a huge cheerleader for these ideas, came

to the concepts kicking and screaming, hoping that he would not have to find a new way of making a living. From the time he wrote his first page-one article for the college newspaper (on how the security guard at the front gate of the campus had squirrels literally eating out of his hand), he was certain he would spend his entire life writing feature stories for newspapers and magazines, supplementing that (even then) meager income by writing books.

And that is exactly how it worked out—for about twenty-five years. Paul started at one of the largest newspapers in the country before moving on to national magazines, while writing books at night and on weekends. Then, newspapers started disappearing, as did magazines—and we don't have to tell you what is happening to the book industry. Eventually, Paul realized the industries in which he spent his life were going away and were never coming back.

Every day since then, Paul has applied the principles of thinking entrepreneurially as he goes about carefully creating a series of overlapping projects to replace the work he used to have in industries that no longer exist, at least in the form he knew. He thought it was going to be depressing and not very lucrative. He was (happily) wrong on both counts.

The second source of frustration was with all the traditional advice out there about the best way to manage your career. You have heard it all. Here are but three quick examples:

➤ Do what you love and the money will follow.

➤ Don't prepare for your next job; prepare for the one after that.

And then there is what passes for conventional wisdom today:

> ➤ We live in a gig economy—so plan on moving from one project to another.

Let's deal with the flaws in each of these recommendations, to show you why we think there is a glaring need for the ALBR model.

The problem with telling someone to "do what you love and the money will follow" is that it may not. Then what do you do?

In the movies, the answer is simple: You persevere and then, just before the credits roll, you are rewarded. But real life is rarely like reel life. Do you pursue your idea, even if you know it is not going to make you a lot of money? Neither traditional career books nor the ones that deal with the economic future ever answer that question. This one will. (See Chapter 6.)

As for "Don't prepare for your next job; prepare for the one after that," the flaw is obvious. Five years ago, store managers at Blockbuster might have been preparing to one day move into the job of their boss's boss—the regional manager. Bankers writing no-documentation loans thought they were on their way to becoming senior vice presidents, and hundreds of newspaper reporters were doing all they could to become senior editors at their papers. And they are all either unemployed or working in a different field today. Planning to get your boss's boss's job assumes that the world is going to be the way it is today five or ten years out. That's a dangerous and, to be blunt, a stupid assumption, as we will see.

Finally, while the "gig economy" concept is appealing, once you understand what it is and accept the fact that we all must get used to the idea of changing jobs—and perhaps industries—fairly frequently, and perhaps supplementing whatever job we have—or end up with—with a side gig, what exactly are we supposed to do to thrive? No one ever tells us.

To solve all these problems—and more—when it comes to managing your career, you need a new approach. And ours starts in an unusual place: *Don't have a career plan.*

WHY YOU DON'T WANT TO HAVE A CAREER PLAN CAST IN CONCRETE (AND WHAT YOU SHOULD DO INSTEAD)

A career plan assumes you know how the world is going to be sixty months from now. As we just saw when we were discussing the career path of Blockbuster employees, bankers, and journalists—and you can add any number of fields to those three—that is neither a good nor safe assumption.

If you don't know what the world is going to look like five years from now, it doesn't make sense to try to predict potential external factors in planning your career. For instance, let's say it's 2009 and you're an associate marketing manager for the Eastern region of a company that makes stand-alone GPS devices (such as TomTom or Garmin). Your bedrock assumption—remember we are talking many years ago now—is that the world is always going to be willing to carry or deal with an extra device, like your GPS, that plugs into the cigarette lighter of a car.

"No car manufacturer is going to want to go to the trouble of offering 'navigation' as a feature, and who could possibly come up with an app that does what we do," you tell yourself. "My future is secure. So, I am going to plan on being a regional manager in two years and head of marketing for my company in five. Yep, that's my plan." Know anyone who has bought a stand-alone GPS lately?

So, are we saying career planning is waste of time? Yes, much of the time it is—at least as typically conceived and practiced.

BUT WHAT DO THE INTERVIEWERS THINK?

Not surprisingly, our advice is not particularly popular with some hiring managers. While they are willing to concede that if you are in a profession that is evolving rapidly, career planning just doesn't make a lot of sense, that's about as far as they are willing to go.

Well, no one associated with this book is a recruiter. But between the three of us, we have hired literally hundreds of people, and our experience has been that if you are looking to discover a job candidate's ambition, personality, values, thinking process, etc., there is a much more direct—and we would argue better—way of finding out than asking the interviewee, "What do you see yourself doing in five years?"

Instead, ask people what they have been (or are now) utterly committed to in their life: "What really turns you on and attracts you almost in spite of yourself? What are the things that you can't put out of your mind?"

What organizations need today—perhaps above all else—is *commitment*. They need people who truly want to do a great job. Who are driven to do so. The best way to find out if someone has that kind of desire and commitment is to ask about times he has demonstrated it in the past.

Does it have to be work-related?

It would be nice, but no. What organizations are looking for is whether you have developed the "muscle" to be committed. To anything. If you have that muscle, everyone will quickly know whether you can become committed to the specifics of that organization and job. If you don't have the "commitment muscle," it will surely be difficult work for you to develop it, and both you and the hiring organization will end up frustrated.

Why not insist that the desire be work-related in general, and tied to your firm in particular? Well, the moment you say, "Tell me why you feel passionate about joining XYZ Corp.," people are going to be tempted to tell you what you want to hear, instead of the honest and complete truth. They are, as a friend of ours who hires for a large corporation says, "going to start blowing in your ear." It's not that they are trying to deceive you. They want to be excited about your firm. They want to convince themselves as much as they want to convince you. So they are naturally going to be doing everything they possibly can to put themselves in the best possible light.

If you find yourself interviewing for a new job, let us underscore something: If you think that talking about your "desires" can seem "unbusinesslike," get over it.

You know, in general terms, what the company is looking for in an applicant. And you know whether you have those skills. But there are lots and lots of people who are smart, excellent problem solvers, good team players, and who take initiative and want to win. It is going to be extremely hard to set yourself apart, if these are the qualities on which you choose to compete.

Talking about your passions and desires will set you

apart. Once you get the gig, it is up to you (and your future boss) to figure out how to channel that passion for the organization's benefit—and yours.

There are exceptions, though. If you want to work in an industry where things are fairly predictable—say, home remodeling—then plan away. The courses and apprenticeships you need to undertake are well known, and so is the career path and the things you need to do to advance. So, simply figure out where you actually want to be in five years, and work backward, just like all the career planning manuals tell you.

But most of the work world is not this predictable. And it is in settings of high uncertainty where traditional career planning is both a waste of time and potentially dangerous. A career plan can lead you into a false sense of confidence, where you fail to see opportunities as they arise and miss signs that the industry is crumbling around you.

You need an alternative. Here's one that will make up the framework for the advice we will be providing throughout this book.

Instead of picturing what your perfect job or career would be and working backward from there, begin with a *direction*, based on a real desire, in which you think you want to go. Then complement that with a *strategy* to discover and create opportunities consistent with your desire.

In other words, *you don't search for the perfect job, you create it—* either within an existing organization or on your own.

Why the radically different approach? That's easy to explain.

In an uncertain world, you simply cannot come close to imagining what a perfect job might be. It's unknowable, especially when you are trying to predict five or ten years out. As we have stressed throughout, the world as we know it can change radically in that span of time. But what is 100 percent known, however, is what's valuable and important to you: Who are you? What matters to you? Is it working in a specific industry? Managing people, or not? Traveling extensively and moving every few years as part of your career in order to gain new perspectives and responsibilities, or putting down roots? The answers to these questions will point you in productive directions.

> Instead of searching for the perfect job,
> why not create it?

Having considered that, what are your means at hand, your talents and skills? Who do you know, and what do you know? How do you get started on concrete actions that are consistent with these desires? Some of those may take the form of looking for a job, but others might simultaneously entail starting something of your own. In either case, as you act, different opportunities will present themselves.

So, as we explained in Chapter 1, the process we are describing looks like this:

➤ Determine your desire.

➤ Take a small step toward it.

➤ Learn from taking that step.

➤ Take another step.

➤ Learn from that one.

You follow this Act. Learn. Build. Repeat. model until you have a job, have your own business, or have achieved your goal. It's not career planning. It's acting your way into the future that you want.

THERE'S PROOF THIS PROCESS WORKS

How can you be sure this approach will work?

Nothing is guaranteed, especially in the unknown. But people have been using the ALBR model successfully forever. Here's just one story. Ours.

You never want to reinvent the wheel, so when we set off to create our last book (*Just Start: Take Action, Embrace Uncertainty, Create the Future*), which was about the best ways for organizations and people to navigate the unknown, we went looking for people who had done it successfully. And we found one group that was better at it than anyone else: serial entrepreneurs—people who have started two or more businesses successfully.

They used the Act. Learn. Build. Repeat. model to start their companies, and we showed in *Just Start* that their approach to navigating successfully through the unknown would work for any business or individual, not just entrepreneurs who want to start their own companies.

In reaction to that statement, people invariably ask: "Even in managing my career or how I make a living?"

It was a subject we had only touched on in our earlier book, but not explored in any detail. So we went back to the serial entrepreneurs and asked them. More specifically, we began sorting through the first 250 in-depth interviews that had been conducted by the

Babson Entrepreneur Experience Lab (BEEL). The BEEL was created to put the voice and the experience of real-world entrepreneurs at the center of an ongoing effort to design, develop, and experiment with new ways to support entrepreneurs and accelerate new venture creation.

We supplemented the BEEL interviews with another ninety interviews with other people who are trying to come to grips with the new economy. And, in listening to all these stories we found—not to our surprise—that the Act. Learn. Build. Repeat. model worked well as people tried to sort out what it was that they want to do with their working lives.

AND THERE YOU HAVE IT

The wholesale changes we have seen in the economy are only going to increase. You may be spared. But don't bet on it. As we said, your job is probably going to disappear in the near future.

The good news is that there are steps you can take today to make sure that if it does, you not only survive, but thrive.

We will see how, in the next chapter.

WHAT WE JUST COVERED— *AND WHAT'S AHEAD*

1. Unfortunately, the winds of economic and workplace change may sweep you out the door.

2. You can hope for the best (i.e., that your industry and company survive and you don't lose your job). But hope is not a strategy.

3. In a world where you can no longer plan your way to workplace success, you need a new approach.

We will be providing it in the chapters ahead. We start, in Chapter 3, with a discussion of why networking won't save you and why you will need to spend a lot of time preparing for your next job (and if you're reluctant to start a business of your own, that planning could be a very good thing).

CHAPTER 3

Don't Bring a Knife to a Gunfight

When you are facing a future that cannot be predicted with any accuracy, traditional approaches for problem solving (e.g., forecasting, planning, in-depth research) don't help you much. You need to acknowledge that and find alternatives. You need a new set of complementary tools. This is the place where we start giving them to you and point out where you could go off track as you navigate the new world of work. (Hint: The biggest obstacle to your future could be you.)

One of the oldest sayings among comedians is "buy the premise, buy the bit."

What they mean is that the audience must believe the setup to the joke; they need to accept the comedian at face value when he says, "A funny thing happened on the way to the theater."

If they do, they'll laugh at what follows. If they don't, they will sit there and poke holes in the logic: "He really met a smart-alecky homeless guy as he walked over to the theater? Why wouldn't he be coming to the theater in a limo? Did he just make this up to get a laugh?"

Either way, there will be silent stares instead of guffaws and clapping.

If you believe the stories that Bill Cosby tells about the interactions with his wife and kids, then you probably think he is incredibly funny. (If you're not familiar with his "serving chocolate cake for breakfast" routine, check out this YouTube video: www.youtube.com/watch?v=zuamlBQ2aW4. You're in for a real treat!) However, if you think Cosby is a single guy—he's not—and is just trying to think of something funny to say by painting himself to be a clueless husband and father, then the bit isn't funny. (And you will be sitting there thinking: "Who the heck would serve his kids chocolate cake for breakfast? Even single guys know better than that.")

Why are we talking about comedians? Well, the entire buy-the-premise-buy-the-bit concept applies to what we are saying here. You have to believe that there is a very real possibility that your current employment is going to utterly vanish, never to return. If you don't accept the premise, you are likely to take half-hearted steps, if you take any at all, to prepare for the future. And worse, those steps are very likely to be down a well-worn path that will lead you nowhere productive, now that the world has changed so radically.

As we saw in Chapter 2, in most cases, picturing where you want to be in five years and working backward from there is no longer the right road to choose when you're trying to create the kind of future you want. You need to be serious about the new approach we are advocating, where you take little steps toward a new goal and learn from taking each of those small, smart steps.

The takeaway from this: To borrow from the title of Marshall Goldsmith's great book, what got you here—to the success and accomplishments you have achieved up until now—is not going to get you there (i.e., where you want to go in the future).

· Your current skills may not hold you in good stead tomorrow. You need to acknowledge that and come up with alternative approaches.

· In other words, you need to find a new set of complementary tools that will *work with* the talents and abilities that you already have, *not replace them*. This is the place where we start giving them to you.

But before we do, let's take a deep cleansing breathe and address one of the things that may be bothering you.

"IT'S NOT FAIR!"
YOU'RE RIGHT. IT'S NOT. GO ON FROM THERE.

We talked to hundreds of people as we went about researching this book, and while we can't honestly say that the majority complained about having to be completely responsible for their careers, a significant minority expressed unhappiness to varying degrees.

We understand. Change is difficult for everyone. And when it is not your choice, it is even harder. You didn't cause the global winds of economic change that are reshaping businesses everywhere, ones that may sweep you out the door.

DEAL WITH IT

You can complain. Whine. Or say what is happening (or soon might) to your career ain't fair. And if you want to do that for fifteen seconds or so, it's fine. After that, own up to the fact that you need to take control of your life and get started shaping the future you want. Complaining, and even thinking about how hard it is to change, doesn't get you anywhere.

If all you do is think about changing, all you will end up with is thoughts about how to change your life. Nothing will truly have happened (other than you will have a few additional thoughts you haven't done anything with).

Action trumps everything.

The first step in changing is knowing exactly where you are. And where you are is probably in trouble—in an industry that is going away or soon might. If you don't understand that, something is terribly wrong. You are going to have to act—probably far sooner than you were planning to.

And of course it isn't fair.

But John F. Kennedy was right. Life is not fair.*

Acknowledge that fact . . . and this one: The odds are better than even money that your job—and probably your industry—is going to change radically. Go ahead; spend a few seconds complaining about it today (while you still have a job) and then start doing something about it (other than hoping that everything will turn out okay).

How do you prepare for this brave new (unpredictable) world? We're glad you asked.

---

* At a press conference in 1962, President Kennedy was asked if it was fair that army reservists, many of whom had previously served on active duty, were being called up to serve in Vietnam. His answer, in part: "There is always inequity in life. Some men are killed in a war and some men are wounded, and some men never leave the country, and some men are stationed in the Antarctic and some are stationed in San Francisco. It's very hard in military or in personal life to assure complete equality. Life is unfair." This is how we feel when people complain about changes in the economy they cannot control. By its very nature, life is unfair.

ARE YOU SPENDING 1,000 HOURS PREPARING FOR YOUR NEXT JOB?

As we've seen, many ways of making a living that once seemed safe can become endangered remarkably quickly, as anyone who rents movies from brick-and-mortar stores or has worked in the record industry or publishing (newspapers and even books, we are afraid) can attest. You could be on the cusp of a disaster and not know it. People inside the eye of a hurricane are often the least able to see all the swirling winds around them.

You'd like to believe you could find another job. Well, as the cliché goes, wishing and hoping don't make it so.

Here's what we conclude: It will take at least something like 1,000 hours—and maybe a lot longer—to recover from a forced career change.

We aren't talking about the time it will take to send out résumés and networking and the like. We are talking 1,000 hours of, in essence, *retraining* to prepare for another job. All the job-hunting-related things you have to do will be on top of that. And they, in and of themselves, are going to take a lot of time. While the best head-hunting firms don't advocate that you spend full time looking for a job even when you don't have one—that is a surefire way to get depressed and burn yourself out—they do advocate devoting twenty-five to thirty hours a week to finding employment. That means you will be spending something like from 8 a.m. to 2 p.m., four or five days a week, looking for work. The 1,000 hours of retraining we are talking about are on top of that.

Let's do a little sloppy math—just for illustration—to show why that 1,000-hour figure is plausible. Your situation will be different, of course, but our numbers will make the point clear.

Let's start with those of us in technical fields. But please note, as we'll show in a minute, people in nontechnical fields are in exactly the same boat. (Ask anyone who used to sell insurance or encyclopedias door-to-door.)

In 1966, students arriving at an engineering college were told that they would be obsolete in seven years. Back then, some people estimated that the volume of information was doubling every seven years—and indeed by 1973 there was, according to some, twice as much information as there was in 1966. Today, the estimate is that the volume of information doubles every eighteen months, and that the doubling time continues to shorten. The trend is clear, even if you don't buy the exact math. It certainly seems we are running harder and harder to keep up with the required knowledge in our specialized fields.

What do you actually have to invest in order to stay in this race? It's a great question, because in this race, information is the tiger and there doesn't seem to be an end to how fast the tiger can run.

But as the old joke* goes, the good news is that you don't have to outrun the tiger. You simply have to outrun your competitors—people like you who are going to be looking for a job, once their industry becomes obsolete.

> If you aren't spending at least six hours a week—
> about an hour a day—preparing for your next
> career, you run the risk of falling behind.
> Start today.

---

* If you haven't heard the joke, here it is: Two guys are in the jungle taking photographs, when they see a lion running toward them. Frantically, one of the men starts putting on his running shoes. Surprised, the other man says, "What are you thinking? You can't outrun a lion!" "I don't have to outrun the lion," he says. "I just have to outrun you."

So, what will it take? If you work in a technical/scientific/engineering-related field—and again, we will be talking to everyone else in a minute—you might start with a simple, rough assumption that three-quarters of your college education will stand you in good stead for your entire life. After all, the basics rarely change. But one-quarter of your education is subject to erosion, and most of that erosion occurs over a five-year period. Said another way, you must recover one-quarter of a college education every five years. (Your situation could be better, or it could be worse. But these numbers certainly feel correct.)

Depending on how much you studied and how much time you spent in class, this quarter time might amount to 300 hours a year—that's about six hours a week.

Hopefully, your job is providing that sort of development. If it is, and you keep at it, you should do fine. You'll gain 300 hours of new and refreshed information and knowledge every year, while the old stuff decays and becomes less relevant. Over four years, you've lost 1,200 hours and refreshed 1,200 hours, so you are okay, provided your training is *not* industry specific. It does you little good to receive constant updates on the best way to repair typewriters if the world has moved on to word-processing programs.

But what happens if your company isn't providing this kind of training? Or worse, you lose your job and the specialized knowledge you have becomes useless. It could easily be that you have a 1,200-hour deficit to make up—just to get back to the level of a recent college graduate. And it could be a lot more than 1,200 hours if you need to change industries.

Do your own math and reach your own sobering conclusions. Odds are you are going to feel—rightly—compelled to begin your training immediately, so you are not forced to play catch-up later on.

Now you might say, "My career hasn't and won't require specialized information like an engineer's job." You may be right. It's certainly true for jobs where your employer can train you quickly, and some firms like Starbucks are really good at this, assuming you want to work at Starbucks.

And it may be true that if you can manage one thing, say, a retail store, you can manage any similar thing, like another retail store. (But this wouldn't be true for an Apple retail store or a computer store or a phone store, or. . . . Most everything these days requires some sort of background and expertise in what you sell or manage.)

If you're working sixty hours a week, odds are you're not spending another six hours on your next move. You're betting on getting ahead in your existing company or industry and thinking that your company will be there to take care of you.

Maybe those are not the wisest bets.

Our suggestion? Find something:

a) That you care about—it will make it easier and far more enjoyable to put in those 1,000 hours—and

b) That might serve as a safety parachute, i.e., could become at least a partial source of replacement income should your job or industry disappear.

Start investing three hours a week in it *right now*. Yes, we know that the math shows you need to put in at least six, but let's be honest. From a dead stop to six hours a week is rather like losing forty pounds—the number is so big you won't start. And more than anything, you need to start. So start small. Trust that as your interest develops, it will be easy to work up to six hours.

What will you be doing with that time?

Certainly, you will be keeping up with whatever new knowledge there is in your field. For those on the scientific/technical side, it will consume a lot of time. For those of us who were liberal arts majors and stayed in nontechie fields, not so much. However, all of us will have to be expanding our field of knowledge and interests, in case our industry (to say nothing of our job) goes away. That means doing everything from mastering the new productivity tools that come along, to forging new relationships with people outside our traditional field of expertise.

But most of all, you will want to start preparing to have more direct control over your economic destiny. (There is a reason we called this book *Own Your Future*.)

In the best of all worlds—i.e., where you get to keep your current job—the new education and skills you gain will make you more energized and allow you to do your job better.

And if the worst happens—your job and maybe your industry go away—you are far better off than all those people who did not make an investment in themselves.

WHY NETWORKING ALONE WON'T SAVE YOU

"Ah," you say. "I understand the argument completely. But you are forgetting one thing, at least when it comes to me. I have the world's largest Rolodex [or the longest list of contacts in my phone] the world has ever seen. Should the worst happen, I'll make a couple of calls and voilà, I will have a new gig with a new company in a relatively short period of time."

You certainly can make that argument. There has been a growing school of thought, which probably dates back more than twenty years to the wonderful books of Harvey Mackay (*Swim with the Sharks* and *Dig Your Well Before You're Thirsty*) and extends through the works of Keith Ferrazzi (*Never Eat Alone* and *Who's Got Your Back?*), that if your network is large enough, you'll be able to rely on it to get out of any situation—including pending unemployment.

But while networking is a good thing, it is not necessarily the answer to guaranteed employment.

Why isn't networking *the* answer? Let us give you four reasons.

1. **You might not be good at it.** We were talking to a fifty-five-year-old friend of ours about how networking is supposedly the best route to go when you are in search of a job or career, and he gave us a response we love. "If that's the case, I will retire now. I suck at networking. I hate to do it. And I won't."

2. **The people you know may be gone.** If you haven't done any networking in a while, you may discover that you know a lot fewer people than you think, despite all those names in your Rolodex or contacts list. People have the bad grace of dying, retiring, or moving on to other fields where they can't be of very much help.

3. **The people you know are in your industry, and the industry isn't hiring.** We don't know about you, but a lot of our friends are in the same fields as we are. (That isn't surprising, of course.) But if your industry is in trouble, then the jobs of your friends (in those same industries) are also in trouble. They probably won't be in a position to do you any good. A good buddy of mine has just been "asked" to leave his high-paid columnist position at a publication whose name you'd recognize. I have known him for better than twenty-five years,

and had lunch with him right after it happened. I could commiserate (and pick up the check), but I couldn't give him the name of a single publication that was hiring that could come close to being able to afford my friend. Such is the state of journalism today. That former columnist negotiated the best deal he could, filed for unemployment, and is writing a probably-not-very-lucrative book as we speak. But the big takeaway is that he is drawing down his retirement savings today, some ten years earlier than he had planned.

4. **The skills that you have may be irrelevant.** The world may have changed radically while you were putting in your fifty, sixty, or seventy hours a week in the past few years.

So, are we against networking? Absolutely not. It can be another resource you can draw on. Just don't depend on it to provide a secure future.

ARE YOU A RELUCTANT ENTREPRENEUR?

That could be a very good thing.

The premise of this book is everyone will have to become entrepreneurial. And some people take to the idea like a Labrador retriever puppy entering a lake for the first time: After about ten seconds of initial nervousness, as they go into the water they are incredibly enthusiastic, and once they are immersed, it's virtually impossible to get them out. (If you are not a Lab owner, ask one.)

These happy swimmers in the entrepreneurial pond are people

who either always wanted to have a business—and had been thwarted for some reason and now have the chance to thrive—or just found a place where they belonged, once they went off on their own.

But do you have to feel that way?

Absolutely not.

You can use entrepreneurship as a means to an end.

Sure, the people who extol entrepreneurship frequently treat the businesses they start as a member of the family. They have an extremely personal relationship with their start-ups. However, you need not feel that way. Many reluctant entrepreneurs end up discovering that starting a business does not lead to fulfillment, in and of itself. They just don't have that gene. But the business does provide them other substantial benefits, such as replacement income, more control over their lives, and seeing a direct relationship between what they do and the end result. And that is pretty darn fulfilling.

FRANCHISEES ARE ENTREPRENEURS

When franchising started to become incredibly hot back in the 1970s and 1980s, there was a tendency among some "serious" businesspeople to refer to franchisees as people who were "just buying themselves a job." The thinking went that these people were plunking down, say, $500,000 for a franchise that would pay them $50,000 a year for the rest of their life, thanks to the efforts of the parent company, and they were just trading their old corporate job for a new one, in slightly different form. Well, the patronizing attitude was wrong.

We could point you to the dictionary definition of an entrepreneur and you could see that it is: "A person who organizes and manages any enterprise, especially a business, usually with considerable initiative and risk." And franchisees certainly fit under that definition. (For those of you who want to quibble about the words *initiative* and *risk*, we will return to that point in a second.)

But you don't need a dictionary. Just common sense. In the for-profit world, an entrepreneur is someone who creates and runs a new business where one did not exist before. And, no, the McDonald's franchisee didn't create McDonald's. But he certainly created a McDonald's restaurant someplace where there never was one before.

But they don't take much risk, you cry. Neither do the most successful entrepreneurs. They don't like risk. They accept it as part of the game and then work extremely hard to reduce it to a minimum. (See our upcoming discussion of "acceptable loss" in Chapter 4.)

Franchisees understand this perfectly. Serial entrepreneur G. Michael Maddock likes to say that "knowledge is learning from your mistakes. Wisdom is learning from the mistakes of others." Franchisees are wise. They sign on after the parent company has (hopefully) made all the major mistakes.

Our point is simple: Franchisees are entrepreneurs.

Someone who wrote in to our website serves as a case in point: "I decided to get involved with an online franchise so I could be my own boss! I wanted to OWN my life and not continue to live as a child when I was an adult. I wanted to dictate my schedule 24/7," he said. "I love what I do because I have mentors who paved the path for me, so I can clearly see the way and build off what they have done."

So don't think you need to be someone who had a lemonade stand or organized a regular neighborhood car wash when you were a kid to be helped by this book. The ideas we will be advocating are universally applicable, and you will benefit, even if you couldn't sell your mother a box of Girl Scout cookies when you were growing up.

THE BIGGEST OBSTACLE: YOU

Let's end the chapter the way we began it. The odds are you are going to have to change your approach to your career, and perhaps even change your career itself. We know. That is a big, sweeping, scary statement.

Here's another. Despite all the uncertainty in the marketplace and all the upheaval in the global economy, the biggest reason you are likely not to thrive is you.

If you insist on treating an unpredictable universe as if it is predictable, the odds say that you are going to get into trouble. Sure, things could work out, if you continue doing what you are doing. Your career could trundle along just fine until you decide to hang it up. But do you want to bet your future on the word *could*?

Now, we aren't suggesting that you eliminate the reasoning that you have used to make yourself a success to this point. For example, we are *not* saying that given all the uncertainty out there, just chuck it all and plunge headfirst into the unknown and pick a new career at random. Nor are we arguing it's time to rush into that new venture you have been thinking about, the one that is not fully formed. (See the sidebar "Entrepreneurs Are the Most Risk-Averse People We Know.")

ENTREPRENEURS ARE THE MOST RISK-AVERSE PEOPLE WE KNOW

Let's pause here and underscore something that sometimes confuses people.

When we argue that everyone needs to become an entrepreneur, we don't mean the cartoonish image the press uses to paint entrepreneurs. If all you knew about entrepreneurs is what you read, you would think they were swing-for-the-fences, bet-everything-on-one-roll-of-the-dice men and women. Nothing could be further from the truth. They are some of the most risk-averse people around. And their attitude is one you should adopt. Before you even think about doing anything new, know exactly how much you are willing to lose.

It's basic risk management. If you are going to compete in an area where there are uncertain outcomes, you never want to pay/risk/bet more than you can afford to lose.

You know what's at risk, of course. Money is the most obvious. But there is also reputation, both personal and professional, and time.

Time is invariably unappreciated. Our suggestion? Just as you have a dollar amount in mind (e.g., I can't afford to lose more than $X), you should have a specific time figure in mind as well (e.g., I can't afford to give this idea more than four months). The reason for that limit is twofold. First, you only have so much time, so wasting it is simply silly.

Second, if you are working on one idea you cannot be working on something else simultaneously. Missing out on an opportunity can be devastating.

When it comes to determining how much you can personally risk in starting a new venture, ask yourself these three questions:

1. What are my assets?

2. What can I afford to lose?

3. What am I willing to lose in the worst-case scenario?

Now, the concept of risk changes as the circumstances do. If you think your job could disappear in the next couple of years, you are (or should be) willing to take on more risk than a college professor who has tenure.

Still, the basic rules apply.

There are two reasons we're not telling you to act rashly (beyond the fact that it would be a very silly thing to do). First, as we discussed in Chapter 1, the traditional way of reasoning—where you forecast the future, construct a number of plans for achieving what you want (before picking the optimal one), assemble the necessary resources, and then go out and implement it—continues to work really well when the future is going to be similar to the immediate past. If you are trying to figure out how to sell an existing product into an adjacent market, for example, you won't need a radical overhaul in your thinking. The way you traditionally solve for this situation may work just fine—and you never want to discard something that works well.

CHANGING YOUR THINKING
(WITH HELP FROM DR. SPOCK)

The people at New Directions, "the life portfolio company" based in Boston, spend a lot of time working with people who, through no fault of their own, are suddenly out of a job. They also engage others who, as the name of the company suggests, want to take their working life down a different path.

New Directions argues that people need to become the CEOs of their own life. It is similar to our position that everyone needs to become an entrepreneur, although there is an important difference. The term *CEO* conjures up the image of a boss directing a staff. Others are doing the work. The word *entrepreneur* evokes the image of you doing a lot of things yourself.

That said, one of the things New Directions does that we really like is point out that while the idea of taking control of your working life can be initially unsettling, you come to the situation with far more skills than you initially may have thought. You may know, for example, how to do everything from writing a business plan to creating positioning and marketing messages, and you can use those skills to market, position, and price yourself as you go out on your own (or to help position yourself for whatever you decide to do next). That means you are probably going to be further along than you thought, if you do go off on your own.

It turns out that Dr. Benjamin Spock was right when he wrote in the first sentence of the classic *Baby and Child Care*: "You know more than you think you do."

Second, what we are advocating is an additional tool. It doesn't *replace* what you've been doing; it works *with* it—especially in situations that are unknown, such as what the workplace will look like in the future.

And that's the point. Assume your job simply won't be there in the near future. We will devote the next chapter to offering suggestions about what you can do in that case.

WHAT WE JUST COVERED— *AND WHAT'S AHEAD*

1. What got you here, won't get you there. You are going to need to develop new skills in order to thrive in the years ahead.

2. You will need to spend something like 1,000 hours preparing for your next career. And that number is over and above all the time you will have to devote to working on your résumé, finding job leads, and going on interviews.

3. Sure, networking will help. But odds are it is not going to save you.

4. If you are risk averse, you could be the perfect entrepreneur. The best entrepreneurs are the most cautious people we know.

5. If you think this career upheaval isn't fair, you are absolutely right. But you still have to deal with it.

How to deal with uncertainty is the subject of Chapter 4, where we introduce the Act. Learn. Build. Repeat. model in detail.

SECTION II

Get Out of the Headlights, Dear

CHAPTER 4

Begin Moving Toward What You Want

While ultimately you will be the judge, of course, we'd like to believe that every chapter in this book is important. But this one is the key to the entire book. And because it is, let us spend a minute or two setting up what you are about to read.

If you had to boil down what we have been talking about to a single word, it would be *uncertainty*. How do you navigate your way toward making a pleasant living doing something you like when:

a) Things are changing radically,

b) You aren't sure where you should be going, and

c) You don't even have a map.

In this kind of situation, it helps to have a role model. And we found one—serial entrepreneurs—people who have created two or more successful companies. There is nothing more uncertain than starting a business and these people are masters at it.

In our last book, *Just Start: Take Action, Embrace Uncertainty,*

Create the Future, we outlined in detail how these entrepreneurs deal with the unknown.* Here, those methods are reduced to a single formula. In short, entrepreneurs do the following:

➤ Determine their desire. That is, they begin by figuring out what really gets them excited.

➤ Take a small step toward finding or creating something that will allow them to capitalize on that desire.

➤ Learn from taking that small step.

➤ Build off that learning and take another step.

➤ Learn from that step . . . and so on.

It's a model that we call: Act. Learn. Build. Repeat.

What works for entrepreneurs will work for you. That's why as you go about navigating your future career from this day forward, you want to take the same approach they do every time they journey into the unknown.

This chapter is designed to show you how to do just that.

SUPPOSE YOU WERE ABOUT TO GO ON A TRIP

We have talked a lot about why figuring out what to do with your working life is a lot harder today than it used to be. We've moved from

---

* *Just Start* builds upon the revolutionary research done by Saras D. Sarasvathy, Isidore Horween Research Associate Professor of Business Administration at the University of Virginia's Darden School of Business, to whom we dedicated our last book. Her research underpins many of the ideas in this chapter.

navigating in an extremely stable environment to moving about in a world that seemingly has no rules. (Note that word *seemingly*, because there are rules. They're just new ones. You will know what they are before the chapter ends.)

To drive home the difference between where we were and where we are now, and to get us started down the path of the best way to deal with this new world, let's imagine two different scenarios.

In the first, you want to get from Washington, D.C. to Boston. Easy, right? You figure out when you will be going—say, next week— and then you start to make any number of practical decisions:

➤ How quickly do you need to get there?

➤ Are there places you want to stop along the way?

➤ What is your preferred method of travel?

➤ Is there a specific time of day you want to go?

You get the idea. You'd plan out your itinerary ("I'd like to stay a day or two in New York City on the way") and determine the best mode of travel for what you want to accomplish ("I think I'll drive") and you plan out a route. Maybe you would use a traditional map or a GPS to chart out your course.

If you get off track—and all the construction around New Haven can make things confusing when they keep moving which side of I-95 to stay on as you travel north—it is no big deal. You double-check the map, reboot the GPS, or even ask for directions and get back on your way.

Now suppose you were dropped into the middle of an Amazon rain forest and you had to get home? You wouldn't do a lot of planning, and the kind you did would be different. You wouldn't be thinking of the sequence of steps—"Let's see . . . once I leave Midtown

Manhattan, I want to get over to the West Side Highway and start looking for signs for I-95 north." In fact, you wouldn't do much planning at all.

You'd take a small step in what you hope is the right direction and then pause and see what you have learned from taking that small step. ("Hmmm. I am still on solid ground and I think I see a sliver of daylight in the direction I am heading. Let me go and take another step that way.")

> The people who are best at dealing with uncertainty are serial entrepreneurs. That's why in navigating your future, you want to take the same approach they do every time they journey into the unknown.

Well, the employment situation is a lot like the two scenarios we just described. Before all the economic disruption we've experienced in the last few years, things worked pretty much like the Washington-to-Boston scenario. The journey was straightforward and stable, and you could take your time figuring out how to get from here (where you were in your career) to there (where you wanted your career to be in the future), since nothing much was going to change in the interim.

Today, the employment search is far closer to being dropped in the middle of the rain forest. You aren't sure where you are or how you can get to where you want to be. In this kind of situation—with uncertainty all around you—the soundest approach is to do what serial entrepreneurs do: Take a small step, learn from it, and build off that learning.

WHERE DO YOU START?

Invariably, when we talk about why everyone will need to master entrepreneurial thought and action, people immediately have questions such as: What specific things will I need to know? How important are my networking efforts going to be? How am I going to get the funding I need if I do, in fact, decide to start a company?

These are legitimate questions all. But they are not the place to begin. *This* is: Ask yourself, what is it you truly want?

Unless you truly want to make something happen, the odds are nothing will. Without that desire, nothing else matters or occurs. Your life will be filled in other ways.

"Phooey!" you say. "There is nothing more important to me than figuring out how I am going to be able to pay the bills, and hopefully have a little something left to put toward retirement."

Okay. We are willing to take you at face value. But the question is this: Are your actions matching your words? Could someone look at how you are spending the vast majority of your days and conclude—unprompted—what it is you want to do with your life, specifically your work life? If she can't, our guess is you are probably not clear on what you truly want to do. You aren't centered on your desire.

When you are faced with uncertainty—and we could be talking about "what should I be doing for work" or "with the rest of my life"—the starting point is this: What do you *want* to create?

You have some sort of idea of what you'd like to bring into being.

That concept could be as vague as "I want to make the world a better place" or "I think I want to work for a company based in Paris," or as specific as creating a new kind of software or starting a different kind of HR consulting firm, one where all the employees are partners.

Any idea you have could be great. But you need to do something to make it a reality. Thinking is terrific, but absolutely nothing happens unless you take smart steps to translate your idea into action. If all you do is think about that idea, all you will have when you are done is thoughts. You have to do something to make those thoughts real.

> You need to put your thoughts into action to see if you are right about there being a potential audience/customer for your idea (and learn what you need to change if there is not). Thinking by itself doesn't accomplish anything.

But the only thing that is going to get you to take that step is desire. People who create something new *wanted* to do it. Often they say they had to do it; they felt compelled. But at the very least there was a desire—to act.

Desire is a word we rarely use in connection with commerce. And when it surfaces, some people are quick to try to eliminate it because it sounds squishy, unbusinesslike, and of course, hard to quantify and teach. But it is the right word. Unless you have an aspiration, a passion, then you are just going to muddle along, invariably settling for the thing that looks easiest at the moment, and we really can't help you.

HERE'S WHY DESIRE
(NOT SEX) IS SO IMPORTANT

Surprised that desire is this important? If you think it through, you will understand why you shouldn't be. On the surface, it seems there are four questions you might ask before starting any new venture:

1. **Is it feasible? That is, is it within the realm of reality?** At least for now, hold off on your plan for that perpetual motion machine that powers itself, or your idea for a diet that will allow you to live forever.

2. **Can I do it? That is, is it feasible for me?** The applicable point: If you are willing to make the commitment to making the seemingly unfeasible feasible, fine. (See one of our favorite movie scenes.*)

---

* If you haven't seen the movie *Love Actually*, you should.

In the scene in question, Sam, age 10, has fallen head-over-heels in love with classmate Joanna, who he is convinced doesn't know he exists. Sam has been struggling to figure out a way to come to her attention.

After an extended period of moping, he has the answer, which he excitedly shares with his step-father, Daniel.

It is a solution as old as time . . . or at least as old as rock-and-roll. He points out that the most desirable girls always seem to fall in love with musicians.

Daniel quickly agrees, pointing out that even Ringo Starr, who was never described as the cute Beatle, was able to marry Barbara Bach, a "Bond girl." (She played Anya Amasova in the James Bond film *The Spy Who Loved Me*.)

It turns out that there is a big concert at the end of the semester and Joanna will be the featured vocalist; and Sam says if he is a member of her backup band, and plays extremely well, she might not only notice him but also fall in love with him.

Daniel agrees the plan is brilliant, but points out the tiniest flaw. Sam doesn't play an instrument. That, says Sam, is a minor, inconsequential obstacle.

Sam does indeed learn a musical instrument—drums—before the show, and backs the girl of his dreams—who does indeed notice him—in the big song in the movie.

3. **Is it worth doing?** Will there be a market for what I want to sell? Is there potential to turn a profit? Will people appreciate what I am trying to do? Will I get the psychic satisfaction I seek? In other words, does it make sense to put in all this effort, either monetarily or psychologically?

4. **Do I want to do it?** It is this last question that matters most. Why? Well, either the venture is something that you want or it's something that leads to something you want. If it is neither of these, there's no reason to act or to answer the other three questions. We'll explain. There is simply no way you are going to give your new venture your full effort if your heart isn't in it at least to some degree. But once you want to do something, everything gets reframed. The negative emotional response to all the unknowns is reduced. The reality hasn't changed. You still don't know what is out there, but you'll find a way around the problem because you care about what you are trying to do.

Let's say you are working for a software company and your boss says he would like you to open several markets in what was formerly part of the Soviet Union. Here's how our four questions play out:

Is it feasible? You haven't a clue. What is the level of computer penetration in the market the boss wants to target? Are the machines people use there compatible with what we have in the States? Is there a distribution network in place that you can piggyback on?

Can you do it? Maybe. Maybe not. You've never done anything like this before. You don't speak the language and you don't have a single contact east of London.

Is it worth doing? Who knows the size of the market and whether it will be profitable? Furthermore, your boss hasn't made it clear whether you can personally benefit from taking on this challenging assignment. Instead of putting your professional reputation on the line, maybe it would make more sense to start having lunch with headhunters?

Do you want to do it? Well, no. It's the boss's idea. And the thought of flying halfway around the world on a regular basis on what may turn out to be a fool's errand is not exactly making your heart beat faster.

Situation #2 is exactly the same, *but you are the one* who wants to sell the software in this new market:

a) It is your product. You have started a company to both develop and distribute it, and

b) you are dating someone who happens to live there.

What's the likely result in both cases? It isn't a hard question.

In the first instance, where desire is *not* part of the equation, you aren't in any hurry to do anything because the situation is so uncertain, unknown, and unappealing. You will keep thinking about what you are up against and search for more data. ("I wonder how Adobe handles these problems? Microsoft? How about the various gaming companies?") After all, it's better to study carefully and make sure all the bases are covered than to launch, have it not work out, and then have everyone say, "You didn't think it through." At best you will take a lot of time, and at worst you will put it at the very bottom of your "to-do" pile, never taking any real action and hoping your boss never follows up, even though the opportunity might have been real.

But, in the second case, the presence of desire alters all of that. Because you want to do it, you are much more likely to take a first, small smart step toward solving the challenge. For example, the next time you head off to Eastern Europe for a romantic week, you set up some appointments with companies that might be able to handle distribution for you.

Here's one last reason that "want to" is so important. Nobody will be committed to what you're doing if they don't see your desire, your belief in your idea, and your willingness to try to accomplish it. As a result, it will be substantially harder to find:

1. Employees to come along with you

2. People to give you financing

3. Customers

So, before beginning anything new, ask yourself this: Is this something I really want to do? If it isn't, you are likely to be happier and more productive spending your time on something else.

ONCE YOU KNOW WHAT YOU WANT . . .
TAKE ACTION

With desire fully present, it is time to move on to the next step in the model. Let's use a snippet from one of our favorite musicals to transition into the first tangible step in implementing our model.

In *A Chorus Line*, Cassie, a great dancer on Broadway, was destined for stardom in Hollywood, according to all the hype surrounding her career. Well, it hasn't worked out that way, she explains, as she recalls her days trying to become an actress:

"Oh, sure [I worked a bit]. A rotten part in a so-so film, a part that ended up getting cut, thank God. I was a go-go dancer in a TV movie of the week. Let's see. Oh yeah, commercials. I almost got to squeeze a roll of toilet paper but I lost out in the finals. Isn't that something? Seventeen years in the business and I end up flunking toilet paper squeezing? And I was a dancing Band-Aid. That was fun.

"As for the rest of my time in Hollywood? We had an earthquake . . . and I got a terrific tan."

Cassie is telling her story to Zach, the director who is auditioning dancers who will appear in the chorus of his new musical. Cassie would like to be one of them. Zach tries to talk her out of it, saying it is beneath her, and Cassie's response is: "God, I'm a dancer, a dancer dances!"

That statement sums up perfectly the Act step in our Act. Learn. Build. Repeat. model. A dancer does indeed dance. She doesn't sit around all day and think about dancing, or just read about dancing, or only talk about dancing. She can do all those things, of course. But she has nothing to show for it, unless she dances. Until she takes action (by dancing) nothing happens—and we would argue, she isn't a dancer.

It's no different for you. You can talk about what a great idea you have for a new business venture. (And indeed it might be great.) Or you could go on with great passion about the idea you think would be perfect for the community, or you could bore your friends to tears with the way to reform whatever it is that is your pet bugaboo, but unless you do something—or something happens as a result of all that talking/thinking/discussing—you haven't accomplished a thing. You (apparently) have the desire, but that's all you have.

You need to take action.

But what kind?

"I know, I know," someone will say excitedly when asked the question. "You spend a lot of time researching and planning. Then you line up the resources you need and then, when you start, you go big."

Every part of that response is wrong.

As we have seen, researching and planning don't help you much when the world is changing as fast as it is. You can come up with a plan that is perfect—for a world that passed you by while you were spending all that time planning. Similarly, you could end up solving a problem that has either gone away or been solved by someone else while you were lining up resources. You see the problem with going big. You could end up missing by a mile.

So, how do you take action? One tiny step at a time.

Let's go into this in a bit more detail.

SMALL, SMART STEPS

You have an idea for the next phase of your career. You think it would be intriguing to finally start that social media company you've been talking about for years, or that concierge-type service aimed at single guys with lots of money but no time.

Whatever it is, great. What's the next step? Well, it is probably not renting office space, lining up partners, and searching for employees who might want to come along with you on this new journey. It's not even writing a business plan. All that comes later (if you need to do it).

No, the first step is to find out if your idea is viable. You want to keep your investment of time, money, and emotional capital to an absolute minimum, just in case what seems like a wonderful idea turns out not to be.

But don't you have to do intensive research to know whether you are on to something? No, not really. At this point, you just want to know if your idea *could* work. It's not like you are launching a new soft drink globally, where you are betting hundreds of millions of dollars. It's more like you are simply trying to find out if people might buy a bottle of pop that tastes tomatoey. (Don't laugh. Dr. Brown's Cel-Ray soda, which does indeed taste, sort of, like celery, has a cult following.)

And you can discover that level of feasibility by simply asking people. You might find that you can't even get them to consider the idea of a tomatoey soda, so you may need to whip up a batch to see:

a) If you can do it

b) If people like it

c) What—if anything—you can do to tinker with the formula, in case they don't

And, oh-by-the-way, it wouldn't hurt to come up with a marketing approach that will get them to at least consider sampling that tomatoey soda, instead of automatically turning up their nose at the idea of a soft drink that tastes like a vegetable.

As you take these small steps you might discover that the new concept you are thinking about already exists. A friend of ours, worried about his future in corporate America (he works for a major department store), was convinced that he had come up with the perfect idea: a website that would literally pay you to shop the way you normally do.

You'd go to his site and type in the store you wanted to shop online, like Nordstrom, or the product you were looking for ("coffee maker"). His site would take you to sites of various retailers that offered what you were looking for, and if you bought something, you would receive a rebate from him.

"Just about every retailer is looking for new customers," our friend explained. "I did some checking and they promised to give me, on average, a 4 percent cut of every purchase someone I referred to them made. If I split that commission with the shopper—giving them a 2 percent rebate—why wouldn't they always log on to my site instead of going to Nordstrom.com or whoever, directly? Sure, I am adding one small step to the shopping process, but I think people will put up with one extra click, in exchange for getting cash back."

He was absolutely right, of course. There was only one small problem. Someone had beaten him to the idea. Mr. Rebates offers a "cash back rebate at over 2,000 popular stores like Best Buy, Dell, JCPenney, Nordstrom, and more." And Mr. Rebates makes money exactly the way our friend imagined he would. "The stores that you see on Mr. Rebates pay us a commission on each sale that is generated. Most shopping-based websites keep that commission for themselves, but we refund a good portion of that commission to you!"

Being beaten to the punch happens more than you would think. In fact, the Urban Dictionary has a term for when you have an idea for a business/website/start-up and find out that it has already been done. The term? You've been "Mr. Skin'd." As in, "I was gonna make a website about slang and street definitions, but I got Mr. Skin'd by urbandictionary.com."* To avoid being "Mr. Skin'd" is another reason you should start small.

---

* The reference is a real website called Mr. Skin, "the largest free nude celebrity movie archive." In the movie *Knocked Up*, underachieving friends talk endlessly about creating a website that will direct people to the "good parts" (meaning nudity) in every movie ever made, only to find out after months of planning that Mr. Skin had beat them to it.

HOW TO GET STARTED

The biggest problem people have with the Act. Learn. Build. Repeat. model is getting started. It seems that Sir Isaac Newton got it right with his First Law of Motion: Bodies at rest tend to stay at rest. Many people just can't seem to get underway and, as a result, they stay at rest.

What does it take to get started?

One easy way is to have someone light a fire under you: "If you don't do X, by such and such a time, you're fired!" Or you light a fire under yourself: "I am not going to sleep tonight until I have taken a first step toward finding a new job."

The problem with lighting a fire under yourself (or having it lit for you) is that eventually your backside gets burned. It's not a great long-term strategy. Once the threat ends, you have no real motivation to continue. And if you are operating in an environment where you are constantly threatened, it gets demoralizing very quickly.

So, what is the best way to get started? Identify:

➤ Something that you want and

➤ Something that you can do about it, with the means at hand (i.e., take an action that is within your level of acceptable loss; that is, the cost is minimal, if the action doesn't work out)

Put that way, there are only four logical explanations for why you are not moving toward your goal:

1. Habit.

2. You don't have the means at hand.

3. The perceived cost is too high. Or

4. You are lying to yourself about what you want.

Let's stay on that last point for a bit. Most people who say they want to get a new job, or meet someone, or lose weight really do want to find new employment, find their significant other, or be thinner. As for overcoming habit, that's "simply" a matter of getting used to taking action. (More on that in a second.)

So this means if you aren't taking action toward what you want, you perceive taking action as being either too costly or too risky.

What's the solution? It seems simple, doesn't it? Reduce the cost and risk to acceptable levels.

That sounds basic . . . and it is. But even so, you might need some help. If you do, here's one easy solution. Talk to a friend about the challenge you face. ("I really want to find a new job, but I just can't seem to get going.") Together, come up with a list of possibilities, being as specific as you can. In the case of the new job, you would identify what you want to do (i.e., start a company or work for someone else, etc.). This could take a couple of conversations, and that's fine. But don't wait until the end of all your talks to get moving. Remember, we are trying to get you out of the habit of not moving.

Let's say at the end of the first conversation you decided your next job will be with another company. So, you immediately start building a list of potential firms to contact and maybe even go as far as talking to people who have the sort of job you want.

At the next meeting, you and your friend would try to come up with a complete list of places that might hire you, as well as identifying whom to contact at those firms.

Then you'd set a deadline—say, within a week—when you will

report back to your friend. At that meeting you'd say what you did to follow up, or explain why you didn't do anything.

Isn't setting this deadline the same as lighting a fire under yourself? Yes . . . but also no. Yes, in the sense that you have drawn a proverbial line in the proverbial sand. But no, because you are acknowledging upfront that you may not take action.

Let's suppose you don't. At the next meeting with your friend, you would explain why you didn't. Maybe it was because you were sick, so you give yourself a pass. But it could be you didn't take action because you found the idea of cold-calling companies too intimidating.

In that case, you and your friend would try to break down the next step into even smaller parts. For example: Is there someone you know who can get to someone she knows at the company? Is it possible to find out if the company takes online applications seriously? If so, you wouldn't have to cold-call.

And so the process would go until you reduced taking the next step to a point where it is doable . . . or you and your friend conclude you are never going to take action, for whatever reason.

HOW THESE SMALL STEPS WORK

So exactly how do you proceed?

To answer that question, let's use a concrete example. Say you want to start a business. (If you don't want to start a business, then simply mentally substitute your idea for finding a job in the following example. The steps will be similar.)

If you have an idea for a new business, sure, you talk to your friends about what you are thinking of doing—in the hopes that they can both shoot holes in your concept and suggest ideas that can improve things.

And you continue to take small steps from there, trying out the concept on ten potential customers to see what they have to say.

But just because you are taking small steps doesn't mean you can afford to be inefficient. You can't. Remember one of our premises is you always want to have enough resources left to fight another day, so you need to expend the minimum as you move as quickly as possible. (See the sidebar on acceptable loss.)

What accomplishes both goals is getting underway with the assets you have at hand. To discover exactly what those assets are, ask yourself:

> ➤ **Who are you?** What traits, tastes, skills, and inclinations do you have that you can draw on in starting a new venture? When you ask yourself "Who am I?" you are trying to find out what kind of a person you are; what kinds of things turn you on; what really matters to you; and what kinds of things you will *not* do because they either go against your values or you just don't find them interesting enough to invest any time in. If you are not happy professionally, odds are you are not going to be happy personally.

ACCEPTABLE LOSS

Let's start at the beginning. Moving into the unknown—and taking your career in a new direction certainly qualifies—involves risk. Given that, you must decide how much you can afford to lose before you get underway; that is, you need to know your "acceptable loss" before getting started.

How do you figure it out? As you prepare to take action,

you need to ask two questions to make sure you stay within the bounds of what you are okay with potentially losing.

1. What can I *afford* to pay to take the next step, and

2. What am I *willing* to pay to take the next step?

Now the costs we are talking about go beyond the financial. In fact, there are at least five classes of assets at your disposal—and at risk:

1. **Money.** This is the most obvious, of course. Getting a new venture up and running can be costly—and you don't want it to be, if you can help it. Similarly, if you want to apply your entrepreneurial skills to a new position within a company that is new to you, the job search can be expensive, and you want to keep those costs to a minimum as well.

2. **Time.** Just as you set a dollar figure that would be "acceptable" to lose, you want to have a time limit as well. For instance, "I am willing to give this idea up to six months to see if it will work."

3. **Professional reputation.** There is nothing wrong with an honest failure. You had what you thought was a good idea. You gave it your best shot. It didn't work out. These things happen and people understand. But if you are seen as someone who doesn't anticipate obvious problems, or who can't conserve resources and use them properly, that failure can seriously hurt you in whatever you try to do next.

4. **Personal reputation.** This kind of loss is similar to a loss of professional reputation, but it hits literally

much closer to home. Losing your standing with those near and dear to you, or within your church or civic group, can be emotionally devastating. Moreover, one of the primary sources of resources for your venture comes from your family and friends, and you certainly don't want to waste their money and have to face them across the Thanksgiving dinner table if you do.

5. **Opportunity cost.** If you are working to start venture X, you cannot be working on venture Y at exactly the same moment, and Y, potentially, could be a far better idea. You want to be mindful of what you are choosing *not* to do. You also want to recognize another form of opportunity cost: the price to be paid for not acting right away—in which case, someone else might conceive and implement your idea. (Recall the Mr. Skin example.) And the price to be paid for inaction—you might spend the rest of your life in a job you hate, or miss a great opportunity to make a once-in-a-lifetime contribution—may be the greatest cost of all. It certainly is emotionally.

Let's see how acceptable loss plays out in practice. Consider John A. Byrne, the former editor-in-chief of *Fast Company* and executive editor of *BusinessWeek*, who decided to go out on his own, once he reached his early fifties.

As an expert on new media and the creator, when he was at *BusinessWeek*, of the most prestigious ranking of business schools in the country, Byrne thought there was an opportunity to combine the two. There was clearly something to be done with helping those people who wanted to get into and

excel in business school and find employment upon gradua-
tion.

When the world was more predictable, Byrne said he
would have taken his severance package from *Business Week*
and used it to fund in-depth research to estimate not only the
size of the market, but all the risks and challenges he might
face (competitors, changing market conditions, demographic
trends, etc.). The more potential risks/challenges he believed
he was up against, the more money he would raise, in part to
offset the uncertainty in his situation. The whole planning
process could have taken more than a year.

As he notes, that would have allowed him to launch more
than one website simultaneously. But between the time delay
and the idea of taking on partners to obtain the funding, that
route was simply not appealing. It would have taken too long
and been too costly.

"Instead, I boot-strapped the operation," Byrne says,
"and even only working on it part-time, I was able to get it up
and running in about four months. I probably spent a total of
$5,000 to design and build a website [PoetsandQuants.com]
and I wrote all the content myself initially. Once I had traffic,
I was able to attract advertising." (Not surprisingly, a great
deal of it comes from the business schools themselves.) And
that has allowed Byrne to create a second website aimed at
people taking executive education courses. A third one,
aimed at law students, has just started.

At no point has he grown faster than his cash flow has
allowed. As a result, he owns 100 percent of a small (but
rapidly growing) new media company—one that has no
debt.

➤ **What do you know?** This includes your education, training, experience, and expertise. You never know where the insight that leads to an opportunity will come from. That is why the mental cataloging of what you know is important. And finally,

➤ **Who do you know?** Who can you draw on right now—in your personal, social, and professional networks—to help this new idea succeed?

Asking yourself these questions will allow you to act more efficiently.

Now, let's move on to the next step in the model.

LEARN/BUILD

What could be more natural? You take a small step toward your goal of, let's say, starting a company in your quest to find stable employment. And then you pause to see what you have learned from taking that step. It's the most logical thing in the world, right?

Yes. But nevertheless, people find it difficult because at least on occasion:

1. **We want to get going faster.** The heck with small steps, we've been heard to say. I have the best idea in the history of Earth. I don't want to take a series of small steps to make it happen. I want to make huge bounds toward the goal and have it be a reality a week from Thursday.

2. **Once we make the commitment, we don't want to adjust** because we will lose momentum. When we are moving as quickly as we want to, who wants to change anything based on what you have learned? It just slows you down. Unless the learning is life-altering (i.e., they truly hate what we have), then full-speed ahead.

3. **Once we make the commitment, we don't want to alter our approach.** Changing could be perceived as admitting we were wrong. If we are changing gears or direction, it means we did not get it right the first time. We don't want to own up to that.

4. **Ego takes over.** Who wants to think we need to rely on others to generate the best ideas?

5. **Aren't we the experts?** This kind of thinking is related to ego. Because of who we are, and the titles we hold/held and all the experience we've had, we are the ones who are supposed to be on top of what's going on in the marketplace. We're the ones who should know how to spot trends early. Incorporating other people's ideas is an implicit acknowledgment that this might not be the case and we don't know as much as we think we do.

6. **We succumb to sloth.** Going back and fiddling with something requires additional work, and sometimes we just don't feel like doing it anymore.

Written down this way, it sure sounds dumb, doesn't it? But all these reasons—and others we are sure you can think of—are extremely real. As you get feedback from your tentative steps forward, odds are you are going to fall prey to at least one of them. You need to guard against cach and every one of these pitfalls because as wonderful as you think your idea is, it is only the marketplace that will ultimately decide whether you are onto something.

FAILURE CAN BE GOOD

The reason you have to guard against all these normal human frailties is simple: Every action you take—and remember, taking action is the first step in our Act. Learn. Build. Repeat. model—causes reality to change. You thought the iPhone accessory you were contemplating might find a market, but it turns out that when you showed the proto-type to fifty people, each and every one of them said, "I need one, now." That got you to go into production faster and convinced you to expand your offering to include other types of smartphones as well.

IF YOU HAVE INSUFFICIENT DATA, CREATE YOUR OWN

Notice what it doesn't say in that headline.

It doesn't say make it up. Or guess. Or choose things at random.

It says that if there is no precedent for what you want—that is, there is no reliable data—make your own. Go out and create some. In other words, don't think about what could happen, or try to project based on your past experiences. Go out and see how the marketplace reacts to your idea.

Will people buy it? (You don't need to actually create the product or service. Show them a sketch; tell them about what you want to do.) Will they want to tell others? Will they want to get involved with what you have?

You will never know for sure unless you create your own data (when none is available). It's the best way we know to navigate your way through an uncertain world.

Conversely, you thought there might be a market for your "gag gifts" (like the cucumber floating in a bottle of vodka that comes complete with its own little sign saying "Here's what it means to be pickled"). But people said a) they weren't funny and b) they were too expensive. Devastating news, to be sure. But it is far better to know that while you are in the prototype stage than gearing up into full production and losing a fortune. (We will be talking more about this in Chapter 5.)

REPEAT

Armed with the learning, you make the appropriate changes, painful though they might be. Here's an example involving a real product. A former colleague was convinced he had a better way to do personal financial planning. He had potential clients fill out a detailed questionnaire at their leisure asking them about their assets and liabilities.

They liked the basic idea, but hated using pencil and paper, so he arranged for them to fill out everything online, trying to keep all his questions as brief as possible.

They liked that, but told him they found his dense questions too confusing, so he set up a second version breaking the questions into their component parts. That also met with their approval, but now potential customers were complaining that the forms took too long to fill out.

So, in version three, he created an "executive summary" section that they could fill out to get a quick snapshot of their financial situation before moving on to the more elaborate versions of the forms.

They like that but . . .

The "buts" continued for more than two years—and resulted in twenty-three separate iterations of the product, some minor, some major—before the product, Direct Advice, finally launched and was called one of the best personal finance programs ever created.

THE ALBR MODEL IN ACTION

And there you have it. The key to acting in the new economy. You:

1. Determine what you want to do.

2. Take a small step toward it.

3. Learn from taking that step and build off that learning until you accomplish your goal, decide it is impossible, or conclude there's something else you would rather do more.

Let's look at an example of ALBR in action.

Shawn Gardner, age 40, works for the Saratoga, California, parks department and loves his job. But he realizes that these days, public employees are not the most popular people around, and with budget cuts always looming, he figures it would be a good idea to hedge his employment bets.

"With the changing economy, there's tons of uncertainty out there. You have to be the one to plan your own future," he says.

But what kind of future?

"I was on a winter break in 2009 and wanted to rent a snowmobile for a couple of hours," he recalls. "Not only was the price—$325—absurd, but they wouldn't provide insurance. I had just bought a house and I wasn't going to risk it if I got into an accident. I had a debate with the rental guy, but he said nobody who rented snowmobiles provided personal liability insurance."

Shawn didn't rent the snowmobile that day because of the potential risk. But he kept thinking about the experience. And on the way home, he noticed how many people had snowmobiles on trailers in their driveways, along with boats, jet skis, and other "grown-up toys."

"I spent about six months researching all this and concluded, based on the median income, that people couldn't afford all the toys they had in their garages and driveways," Shawn says. "They'd buy a boat with a home equity loan, and then all of a sudden the value of their homes fell or they lost their jobs, [so] they really couldn't afford to have it."

During the Great Recession, a lot of people sold their toys, and the price of boats and motorcycles fell by 50 percent, leaving those who still had theirs feeling even worse about their purchase.

Clearly, there was a mismatch in the marketplace. You had people who wanted to rent these grown-up toys as opposed to own them. (The upkeep on boats is substantial, and even if things like jet skis are relatively easy to maintain, do you really want your money tied up in owning them, if you are only going to use them a couple of times a year? A jet ski runs about $10,000 to $12,000 new, and people tend to buy them in pairs.) But while you had potential demand, potential renters like Shawn thought the average rental price was way out of line. Jet skis typically rent for more than $100 an hour.

Conversely, you had people who didn't want to sell their toys, but they sure would appreciate some extra income.

Hmmm.

WALKING THROUGH THE MODEL

Shawn saw the opportunity, and it turns out he followed the ALBR model exactly. Did he have the desire to make it happen? Yes, on two accounts: Not only was he worried about the security of his day job, but he is "into power sports."

As for the small steps, he had already done some research that showed that a significant percentage of the people who owned boats, jet skis, and snowmobiles were in over their heads financially and could use the extra cash that renting could provide and they were interested in loaning out their stuff. The next step was to talk to potential renters.

When he did, Shawn realized he had a lot to learn before he could create a successful company to fill the hole in the marketplace. For one thing, promoting the business wouldn't be as easy as he thought.

"Google word advertising won't get the attention of our market, I found out," Shawn says. "Many of our customers—both renters and the people who rent [out their power sports vehicles]—are not necessarily looking online for products. We also discovered that we needed to build relationships. The people who rent their stuff want to know it will be taken care of."

That's why offering insurance was important, as Shawn assumed it would be, but so was a rating system where people—both renters and the people renting their stuff—could comment on the person they interacted with.

Shawn also learned that potential renters needed help in determining what they should charge. Obviously, owners want to get as much as they can, but high prices scare off potential renters. He suggests that people looking to lend out their toys look around and see what traditional rental companies are charging and price theirs at a substantial discount. On average, he says, owners he works with charge 50 percent less.

Shawn's company, which takes a 25 percent commission for handling the transaction, has now moved out of the beta phase and is looking to expand beyond its California base.

WHAT WE JUST COVERED—
AND WHAT'S AHEAD

1. The people who are best at dealing with uncertainty are serial entrepreneurs. There is nothing more uncertain than starting a new business and these people are masters at it.

2. Serial entrepreneurs always take the same approach when dealing with the unknown. They figure out what they want, take a small step toward it, see what they learned from taking that small step, and build off that learning.

3. What works for them will work for you, too, as you try to figure out what you want to do next.

Next, in Chapter 5, we will teach you how to think and deal with the obstacles that may get in your way.

CHAPTER 5

Obstacles Welcome

As you move into the unknown, just about everything you encounter is an asset or an opportunity—even if it is negative.

Really.

We aren't big on clichés like "Every time God closes a door He opens a window," or "There are no such things as problems, only opportunities."

That said, people who succeed at work and in life really believe and act as if "everything is a gift." Well, maybe not every single thing imaginable. But assuming that everything *is* a gift is a good way of looking at the problems and surprises you'll encounter in any endeavor, such as getting a new venture off the ground or finding a new job where you can put your (entrepreneurial) skills to work.

Why take this seemingly Pollyannaish approach? There are three reasons.

First, you were going to find out eventually what people did and did not like about your idea. Better to learn it as soon as possible, before you sink more resources into it. (See the sidebar "Some $500,000 Later.") As we have said throughout, you always want to keep potential losses to a minimum. That means it's far better to learn in the prototype phase that neither flip phones nor videocassette recorders (to exaggerate to make the point) are going to be making a comeback any time soon, than to learn that fact after you have invested a lot of money, time, and other resources.

SOME $500,000 LATER: NEVER MIND (FOR NOW)

It's a painful point, but one that we need to stress. Sometimes your idea just doesn't work out—no matter how big the market need you have identified.

This is something that AnnMarie McIlwain knew going in.

McIlwain is clear about what the future will look like, and while her vision is similar to ours, it is also different. "Everyone should not become an entrepreneur, because the skill set is not universal," she says. "But many [people] will need to become self-sufficient as solo practitioners, which is how 80 percent of all small businesses in the U.S. are characterized, if they want to survive in this economy. We have nearly 20.6 million people who are underemployed and 3.9 million jobs available. Yet lack of work will force many to dig deep and rethink their professional existence."

She is one of those people. "I have always wanted to be an entrepreneur," says McIlwain, who has worked at J & J and P & G. "My husband's job loss at the start of the recession inspired my business, CareerFuel.net." The firm offers one-stop shopping for people looking to change jobs. There are sections on her website for finding a job, starting a business, and getting inspired.

But the website is not where she put her focus initially. From the beginning, McIlwain envisioned CareerFuel as a multimedia company, and when she began pursuing where to begin she noticed a glaring hole in the marketplace. Of the hundreds of cable television channels available, not one is devoted full-time to the care and feeding of our careers.

She figured a cable TV network was the place to start. McIlwain worked on creating twenty-four-hour programming while figuring out the best way to get the various cable and satellite providers to agree to carry her channel. She met with the people who ran those outlets, of course, but she also got members of Congress to write letters saying why such a channel was needed (with the implicit message that the service providers should carry it). Her campaign was thorough, and initially effective.

But, as McIlwain got closer and closer to the launch date, the market starting moving away from her. "The pressure started growing to reduce the number of channels on the air, not to increase them," she says. "It was going to become progressively more difficult to sell the idea of adding another channel to the various cable and satellite systems."

And so despite a $500,000 investment—primarily made from her personal funds—she has switched her focus. For now.

"Sure, it was a difficult decision" to put off launching the cable channel, she says. "But it was the right one."

Knowing when to stop is a key bit of wisdom you acquire as you go about following the Act. Learn. Build. Repeat. model.

Second, the feedback could take you in another direction, or serve as a barrier to your competitors. You thought you wanted to start an online social networking site for preteens. It turns out the universe was bored with that idea, since there were already a number of well-established sites out there and it would be extremely difficult to improve on what they offered. But if you could provide online tutoring for preteens and adolescents in high school? People could be lining up to give you their credit cards.

Third, you got evidence. True, the outcome was not what you were expecting or even wanted, but it still put you ahead of the person who is just thinking about doing something (like opening another social media site aimed at kids). You can move on and try something else (like that online tutoring service).

The thing to remember is that successful people work with what they have at hand—and with whatever comes along—and use it to achieve their goals. And that is why they are grateful for surprises, obstacles, and even disappointments. It gives them more resources (or at least more information) to draw on. It's similar to the approach Japanese manufacturers take. They consider each defect they uncover to be a "treasure," since it enables them to improve their production process.

You see this all the time, when it comes to personal disappointments. Someone suffers a heart attack and is put on a restricted diet. The patient can't find foods he likes to eat, and so he starts a business that provides meals and dining choices to people like him. Or a young mother, feeling frustrated by her new baby, invents something that keeps her baby amused for five minutes, and turns that product into a successful small company that serves other parents and children.

And this experience is not limited to strictly business situations. Parents lose a child to a horrible disease and vow to spend the rest of their lives raising money to find a cure, so no other mother or father has to suffer. Similarly, people who have loved ones killed by drunk drivers or gun violence have created entire social movements designed to eliminate the problem.

The point is that people learn from and capitalize on setbacks large and small, all the time.

One entrepreneur wrote in to our website to share a wonderful story about how he prospered from a small setback:

"I made one of my biggest mistakes very early on when I was still in school, working at RadioShack. It was a mistake that made a big impression on me, and one I have chosen to repeat—yes, repeat—throughout my career and my life.

"A woman, who was probably in her late sixties, entered the store with what appeared to be an old flashlight. I approached her, told her my name, and asked if I could help her. She told me her flashlight was no longer working and that she needed a new one. I said we had a variety of flashlights for sale and that I would be delighted to show them to her.

"As I directed her across the store, I asked if I could see her old flashlight. Upon opening it, [I saw] the problem was easy to identify. Corrosion had fouled the battery contacts. I asked her to wait a moment as I scraped the contacts clean with a letter opener. I replaced the batteries and screwed the flashlight back together. Lo and behold, the flashlight now worked perfectly. I explained what I had done and returned the old, now-working flashlight to the woman. She was elated . . . and I felt pretty good, too." After what seemed like an embarrassing number of thank-yous, the woman left the store with her working flashlight in hand.

"Proudly I turned around, only to be approached by my visibly upset manager. Quite firmly, she explained that we were in business to sell flashlights . . . not fix them. Had I not fixed the flashlight, the woman would not only have purchased a new flashlight, but most probably batteries as well. She reminded me that, as a result of my actions, a sale was 'lost.' Her comments made a big impression on me—particularly juxtaposed so closely with the delight experienced just minutes before.

"Today, decades after I fixed that flashlight, I hold that lesson very dear. However, I don't think that store manager would endorse my interpretation. Since that summer, I have fixed many 'flash-lights.'" Not one of them *ever* failed to ultimately generate returns far in excess of the costs of the "parts," because the entrepreneur has been able to convert countless one-time buyers into lifetime customers.

MISTAKES? YOU'LL MAKE A FEW

This point is so obvious, we almost didn't include it.

At the very heart of the Act. Learn. Build. Repeat. model is the fact that you are going to make what, by any objective measure, are going to be mistakes. You thought people would be clamoring for your Portuguese/Brazilian/Cuban fusion restaurant idea. They weren't. You were absolutely convinced that your blog on the inner workings of the investment banking industry would be hot . . . and the response never got beyond room temperature.

Throughout the book, we have pointed out that these less-than-wonderful responses are a good thing. For one, it stops you from making any further investments in a losing proposition. For another, you learned something, and that new understanding could take you in another direction. (You might offer ethnic takeout dinners instead of opening an actual restaurant or, in an effort to make the blog idea profitable, you decide to charge each of the 1,000 readers who desperately need the information you provide $5,000 annually for finding out what only you know.)

So, we argue, that initial failure is actually something you should embrace. And you should.

But at the moment when people tell you that they don't like your original restaurant or blog idea, their comments are devastating. No one likes bad news, and your first response isn't going to be, "Oh, good. I've learned something that I can apply next time." Rather, you think, "Why did I waste all that time, money, and effort. How stupid could I be?"

Chris Kilbourn knows all about mistakes. As he told us, "Here are my biggest: starting a company with a short-term business model and small margins. Starting a company that was not scalable. Hiring my first employee when I didn't need one. Waiting to start a PR campaign until we had negative press. . . ."

We all understand about mistakes. We've all been there. We know how demoralizing that initial rejection can be.

Nobody likes to fail. Nobody likes to hear "No," or "That's a dumb idea." Nobody likes to put in effort only to be rebuffed. But, it is part of the process, unfortunately. Knowing that helps (at least in the long term).

Someone we know who sells extremely high-end products (and receives a wonderful commission on each one sold) did the math one day and realized that, on average, for every 100 people he pitched, only five said yes. (The actual math was one out of 22 presentations that he made eventually led to a sale.) As a result, every time he got turned down, instead of being depressed he said to himself something along the lines of "Now, I only have to approach 21 (or 20 or 19) more people to make a sale."

> Failing is an important part of the Act. Learn. Build. Repeat. model. Unfortunately.

We try to keep that thought in mind, when people turn us down, and we remember these two thoughts as well:

1. This rejection is part of the process (darn it). And

2. It is also the reason we make small bets (so the losses are not so painful).

It helps. A bit.

And we found that this comment from Kirk Yu, an entrepreneur who shared his story on our website, also makes us feel better every time something does not go our way. He wrote: "Even in that darkest time, we always have the capability to change our situation. It only takes believing in ourselves (and personally, I believe in God as well)."

WANT TO SUCCEED MORE? YOU'VE GOT TO FAIL A LOT

The headline is not as oxymoronic as it first appears. If you consider the old cliché "no risk, no reward," you will understand.

Investing serves as a case in point. Yes, you can get guaranteed rates of return (i.e., your investments won't fail or even fall in value) through things like CDs and money market funds. The problem, of course, is your returns won't be so wonderful. During the last few years your returns on these conservative investments did not keep up with inflation. As a result, you lost ground and buying power.

Conversely, a portfolio made up of 70 percent stocks and 30 percent bonds will (using round numbers) generate a negative rate of return one year out of four on average, but even factoring that in, overall it will give you a return of about 9 percent annually, which is three times what money markets traditionally have yielded.

So, most long-term investors are willing to risk the failure (the down years) for the chance to benefit from the upside.

Venture capitalists understand the concept of failing as well, and take this approach to a whole new level. They are more than willing to have eight or even nine out of ten of their investments lose money, in order to have the chance at a huge winner like a Google or eBay.

Now, when they talk about failures, the innovation experts aren't talking about plunking down a huge sum of money on one roll of the dice. They are advocating making a number of small bets to see which one will pay off.

The same is true for serial entrepreneurs. They don't think of themselves as risk takers, even though everyone else does. They have developed terrific ways to limit potential losses as they start a new venture, as we saw earlier, in Chapter 4 when we discussed how they take small steps.

There are two nice things about taking this approach. The first is that you are never out what is, for you, a painful amount of money, should things not work out as you planned. By definition, you were only risking what you could afford to lose. Second, you get more turns at bat. Because you are not betting everything on one roll of the dice, you have more money to experiment with—and that means your chances for success increase. You increase your odds of success.

So, as strange as it sounds, if you want to succeed (more), you need to be failing (a lot) more.

THE SECOND-BEST ANSWER IS NO

Yes, of course, you want to hear "Yes."

Yes—you got the job, made the sale, your idea is approved, the marketplace loves what you have to offer.

But that doesn't always happen.

However, when you hear "No" (no to the sale; can't use it; don't like it; don't like you), you don't want it to be devastating emotionally—and especially not financially.

Let's say you want to develop a truly killer software program. You could research the market forever; spend months putting together the perfect team; then spend as many months (or longer) gathering the investors (and/or family and friends) you will need to come up with the $2 million or so that it is going to take to get your program to market. And eventually you offer the World's Greatest Software Program for sale.

Or, on the very day you're thinking of creating that program, you can begin by asking potential customers what they think. ("Hey, if I built a software program that did A, B, and C, do you think you would give it a try?")

You learn from that small step: For example, people may tell you that there are an awful lot of great software programs out there that do 80 percent of what yours will, and they are not sure the world really needs what you plan to offer.

At that point, you could simply give up, or head in another direction. ("Just about everyone who had doubts about what I was planning to sell also told me there is a market for a program that does X, Y, and Z. Hmmm.")

Either way you learned quickly. And even if you "failed" (i.e., decided not to create that software program), you did so at little, or in this case virtually no, cost.

That means you have the resources to try again—something that person who raised—and lost—$2 million might not be able to say.

All this explains why the second-best answer is "no." It's far, far better than "maybe," which can have you spinning your wheels. "No" allows you to try something else. "Maybe" keeps you in suspension.

WHAT HAVE WE LEARNED?

What are our takeaways? We have three:

1. If you are faced with a pleasant surprise (for example, more people liked your idea than you could have ever imagined), simply proceed down the path you were heading—although you might want to move a bit faster to make sure the opportunity window doesn't close.

2. If it is an unwanted surprise, treat it as a gift and accept it wholeheartedly. It gives you new information, new evidence, that your competition does not have. Solve the problem, if you can. If you can't, see if it points to an opportunity, or make it an asset (and build it into your offering).

3. Attitude is key. If you assume everything, even a problem, is a gift, it invariably will be.

WHAT WE JUST COVERED— *AND WHAT'S AHEAD*

1. The most successful entrepreneurs treat problems and obstacles as opportunities.

2. Those successful people aren't being naïve. They know they are eventually going to find out what people do and don't like about their ideas, and it is better to learn that quickly. The market feedback could suggest other opportunities, in addition to providing real evidence.

3. Mistakes are simply part of the learning process. The "secret" is to make sure that they don't cost you too much and that you do, in fact, learn from each one and build that learning into the next step you take.

In the next chapter we will talk about what could be a self-imposed obstacle: thinking you have to choose between love and money.

SECTION III

Where Do You Want to Go?

CHAPTER 6

Choosing Between
Love and Money

It is only natural, as you start thinking about your options, to want to do something you love. But what if that something is not going to be profitable? Should you do it anyway?

As you cast about for ideas for what you should do, invariably this question, put to us by one of the readers of our blog, is going to come up: "What should I do if I have to choose between love and money?"

"If you're really passionate about what you do, but it's not going to make you a lot of money, should you still do it?"

It's a terrific question. Let's deal with it now.

It seems like just about everyone who has ever addressed a graduating class of high school or college seniors has said, "Do what you love, the money will follow." That's clear and inspiring, of course. But suppose it's wrong. Suppose doing what you love doesn't lead to riches. Heck, suppose it doesn't lead to you being able to make the kind of living you want. Then what do you do? After all, it is more than possible, as the question implies, that you could do what you truly care about and very well go broke.

OWN YOUR FUTURE

So, what do you do when you have to choose between love and money?

As we talked about in Chapter 4, when you're heading into the unknown, desire is all-important. You simply want to be doing something that you love, or something that is logically going to lead to something you love, in order to do your best work. That desire will make you more creative and more resourceful, and will help you get further faster.

And it will help you to persist. When you're attempting something that's never been tried before—whether it is beginning an unusual project at work, trying to get a new business off the ground, or "simply" starting a new initiative for your town—you're going to face a lot of obstacles. You don't want to be giving up the first time you encounter difficulty. It's why you want to love—or at least deeply want—whatever it is you set out to do. That desire will keep you going when you are faced with the inevitable hard times.

But, let's be real. None of this guarantees wealth, or even financial success. A friend of ours was hanging out at a bar with some fellow professional musicians after a recording session, talking admiringly about another musician they all know and how fortunate it was that "his music was commercial." In those four words, you will find an enormous truth. We all have *our music*, and there is no guarantee that anyone will buy it. Absolutely none. We may love the music we make, we may work extremely hard to bring it to as many people as possible, and be proud of it beyond belief, but it simply may not be commercial. They are two entirely separate things.

So, let's say you think: "I have the desire, but I am pretty certain it's not going to lead anywhere that's monetarily profitable. Now what? Should I still go ahead?"

Of course you should.

Now let's qualify the answer a bit: If you can't afford to do the thing you're passionate about—for example, if you do it, you won't be able to feed your family, or it would keep you from sending your kids to college (which is something you think is more important than whatever it is you're passionate about)—then no, you'd better not bet your economic life on it. As we have seen, one of the fundamental principles concerning how you should deal with an unknown future is that every small smart step you take should leave you alive to take the next small step. So, make sure you attend to your basic needs of food and shelter and the like, before you do anything else.

But even this doesn't mean you can't work on your passion a little—even if it's just for fifteen minutes a day. And you should!

Why?

Research shows that people who make progress every day toward something they care about report being satisfied and fulfilled. (See "The Power of Small Wins," by Teresa M. Amabile and Steven J. Kramer, in the *Harvard Business Review*, May 2011.) Who's not in favor of people being happy?

And we're also in favor of provoking people into pursuing happiness. The nice thing about the reader's question is that it might get people who have—by any objective standard—more than enough money to consider whether they want to continue to do things that are not making them happy, just because going down the current path will make them richer. More often than not, these people say, "Once I get enough money, I'll do what I really want. I won't have to worry about the money." But somehow, they never get to that point.

Time is finite; the question about choosing between love and money might be enough to get you to reconsider how you're spending it.

And of course, the assumption embedded in the question could be wrong. Even though you currently think you won't, you might indeed end up making money if you engage with your passion.

Remember, the future is unknown. Who knows what people will buy, or what you might invent after your very next act? At any given moment, you are only one thought away from an insight—an insight that can change everything.

So take those small steps. You might discover that your passion does, in fact, make you money. After all, who knew you could make huge sums figuring out a way to connect all your friends (Facebook) or make a better map (pick your favorite GPS tool) or sell a different kind of cookie or barbecue sauce?

And even if you don't make a windfall, you still want to spend part of your day, every day, doing at least one thing that's making you happy. Otherwise, something is terribly wrong.

IT IS NOT EITHER/OR

Typically, people ask, "What do you do when you have to choose between love and money?" We prefer to reframe the question before answering it. Here's the way we reword it: "Do you have to choose between love and money?" Here's why we like our question better.

First, it recognizes that you have to make a living. We love the Alan Jackson song "Livin' on Love (Buyin' on Time)," but you can't literally live on love (unless, of course, you marry someone very, very rich). No matter how smitten you are, one (or both) of you has to do something at some point that will allow you to pay the rent.

Second, it allows you to answer the question in a way that is not binary. Invariably when you post a question about love and money, people think the solution is one or the other. When some variation of the question is posted online, people will go on for paragraph after paragraph about how money cannot buy you happiness and anyone who tries is doomed to spend life like Scrooge McDuck, counting his gold coins over and over again and being miserable. We have always had our doubts. Did you ever see the owner of an NFL team on the sidelines on a Sunday afternoon? He looks pretty happy to us.

The choice does not have to be either/or. You can devote most of your days trying to come up with the money you need to live, using whatever free time you have to work on something you love.

Third, the reworded question recognizes that things that you do strictly for love can become profitable ventures. (Recall the afore-mentioned Facebook example.) In other words, when you are asked the question—love or money?—you may not have to choose. You may be able to answer: both.

As we've said, when you are facing the unknown (and we would put the question of whether love or money is better in the "unknown" category) the only way to find out anything for sure is to act. When you're dealing with uncertainty—and whether you are going to make any money from your passion at this point is definitely uncertain—act.

In other words, when you are dealing with the love/money equation, don't assume anything about the outcome. Don't think about what might happen, or try to predict the outcome, or plan for every contingency. Just take a small step toward making it a reality and see what happens.

And as you are taking those steps, keep these three things in mind.

1. The investment it takes to prepare to do something you love or do something you hate is exactly the same. You can quibble with the numbers if you want, or point out that medical school costs more than law school, but the price of your education

and preparation is going to be more or less constant. Why wouldn't you want to be happy once you are done?

2. The same holds true for the cost of starting a business you love vs. one that you hate. It is going to require the same amount of time, money, effort, and the like.

3. It is costly to start over. It is one thing to begin again if your industry suddenly disappears. It is quite another if you wake up one day and say, "I hate what I have chosen to do for a living."

WHAT WE JUST COVERED—
AND WHAT'S AHEAD

1. Do what you love, and the money will follow is perhaps the number-one piece of advice given to graduating students. It's wrong. Money may not follow.

2. You may not have a choice. If you can't afford to do what you love, there is nothing to decide. You don't do it.

3. But if you have a choice, then pursue what you love, even if it's just for a few minutes a day.

In the next chapter we will discuss how you can create your own job.

CHAPTER 7

Creating Your Own Job

The reasons people start companies are as unique as they are, but they seem to fall into nine broad categories. Our guess? You could probably find yourself fitting easily within one of them.

From a distance, successful entrepreneurs can seem like a different species. All we see is their success running an enterprise, and for some people that can be daunting. These intimidated folks are simply not convinced that they could do it, too.

But if you look at the reason why those entrepreneurs started their business in the first place, it readily becomes apparent that most of us have something in common with them. And once that realization hits, it becomes far easier to imagine being in charge of our own enterprise—even if it is "only" a part-time thing.

With that by way of background, let's visit the nine most common reasons people start companies.

REASON 1:
FEAR OF BEING OUT OF WORK

Is pending or potential unemployment enough of a reason to become an entrepreneur (or to at least start looking for ways to apply entrepreneurial thought and action)? In the course of researching this book, we heard from scores of people who said it was. This comment from Zalmi Duchman is representative:

> "I started my business, The Fresh Diet, because I was about to be out of a job (I was working in real estate in 2005 and could see that the bubble was about to burst) and I did not want to have to find a new one. I was twenty-five with a four-year-old daughter and a son on the way. I was in no position to be unemployed, but I couldn't imagine having to work for someone new."

Duchman had noticed that services that delivered three meals and two snacks a day to people who were either on a diet or were too busy to cook for themselves had begun in various parts of the country, but there were none serving the Miami market where he lived. Even though he knew nothing about the food business, he decided to fill that gap:

"I launched my diet delivery website in November 2005 and on January 1, 2006, I delivered meals to the three clients who had signed up and had prepaid. Today, I am thankful that I had the drive to become an entrepreneur and the want to be my own boss. My company now operates five kitchens around the country delivering meals to over 4,000 clients every day."

WHAT WOULD HAPPEN IF YOU WERE FIRED TOMORROW?

The reactions we got when we asked ten people at random the question in the headline were exactly the same.

First, there was some sort of joke. ("Hmmm. I got fired? I

guess that's what happens when you tell the boss she's a jerk.")

Then there was the quasi-denial: "It's not going to happen. I am not going to get fired—I think."

And finally, nine out of ten said, "I just don't know." (The tenth person said they would take early retirement.)

Do you have an answer? Do you know what you would do if you got fired tomorrow?

If you don't, let us suggest a plan that you can start putting in place right now.

1. **Save some money.** Creating an emergency fund is the first step in any plan—financial or otherwise. And we wholeheartedly endorse it. Not only will it allow you to pay your bills, should you lose your job, but it will also give you some breathing room as you figure out what you want to do next. You won't have to scramble quite as much or take the first employment offer that comes along. Speaking of that . . .

2. **Start preparing for that second job today.** As we discussed in Chapter 3, it will take something like 1,000 hours—and maybe a lot longer—to recover from a forced career change. All the work you spend looking for a new job will be on top of that. The 1,000 hours is just the retraining component. That's a long time. Which leads us to our next suggestion as you start preparing for your next job . . .

3. **Find something that** a) you care about—it will make it easier and far more enjoyable to put in the time, and

> b) should you get the pink slip tomorrow, might serve
> as a parachute.
>
> You can hope that you will never have to pull the rip cord,
> but if you do, you'll have an answer to the question of what
> you would do tomorrow if you got fired today.

While the overwhelming need to be able to pay the bills is certainly enough to get you started, we found in the course of interviewing people who became entrepreneurs—either willingly or otherwise—that there were eight additional reasons people started their own companies.

REASON 2:
SPOTTED AN OPPORTUNITY

"I am a physician—anesthesiology and pain medicine specialties," begins Erica Escorcia.

"When the health reform debate started, I really felt the need/obsession to do something that would revolutionize the way care is given, make it more efficient, accessible, and engaging, and decrease costs all at once. I partnered with a relative of my husband, a biomedical engineer, to form Interactive Healthcare Solutions. We use sensors to help patients with neck and low back pain."

The sensors monitor not only how often the patient exercises—a key part of their rehabilitation—but how well they are progressing. Is range of motion increasing? Can they do a little bit more each day?

"We want patients to be able to prevent and treat problems without being confined to only the twelve sessions that insurance plans typically cover," Escorcia says. "With our approach, patients can follow a home exercise plan for long-term success and, hopefully, avoid unnecessary surgery. If surgery is necessary, our system can help rehabilitate the patient as well.

"I was compelled to do this for various reasons. One is survival of my specialty. Pain management is constantly under scrutiny by the insurance companies. They want to see tangible improvement and not read reports that contain what they consider to be subjective comments like the pain is better or it is worse. The sensors provide that hard data.

"Two, the realization that therapy is a continuum of care, not an episode. To truly rehabilitate, sessions must be done for extended periods and with consistency. If insurance only pays for twelve sessions, then that's the maximum number that most people will do. There clearly was a need for what we offer.

"Three, frustration at seeing patients go through therapy only to give up their maintenance after their formal sessions (i.e., the ones that were paid by their insurance plan) were done, and then come back with recurrences. What a vicious cycle—and a waste of resources. Again, this was a huge need.

"Four, interest in helping people develop a true wellness program with long-term monitoring/coaching."

REASON 3:
LIFE IS MORE THAN MONEY

The third reason for starting a company? You believe employment is more than a paycheck. As Daquan J. Oliver wrote in to our website: "I see no value in being just another employee in the world, settling for the realistic and basic over legendary and great."

That feeling was seconded by Abhishek Daga, co-founder of Thrillophilia *("Boundless nature is our inventory. Experiential holidays is our core competence")*, the "biggest adventure travel portal of India."

"I was born to do adventure!" he says. "After I graduated from IIT [Indian Institute of Technology], one of the finest colleges of India, I worked for Cisco for four years but then I changed my mind-set. I realized I just can't live without innovation. Each day I had an urge to create something new, or optimize things.

"Combining my passion for outdoors and my skills of digital marketing and strategy, I started Thrillophilia.com, India's biggest adventure portal and curator. We traveled across India, gathered the firsthand information about the adventures that are available, and met local service providers and brought them online.

"Here's how the idea started. One day I was sitting with friends and discussing the most exciting things one can do in life, and we talked about diving, skydiving, etc., but the discussion did not satisfy me. I thought all the things we talked about gave only a few minutes of adrenal rush. My question was, How could I have this feeling every moment of every single day? And a few days later I realized nothing can be more adventurous than starting your own venture. What bigger adventure could there be than starting your own company?"

REASON 4:
YOU WON'T WORK FOR SOMEONE ELSE

Another reason people start companies? They got mad at their boss.

"After 9/11, the tech bubble, and outsourcing, finding a good IT job was hard," Manny Mamakas recalls. "I was a skilled network engineer with an electrical engineering background and still I was out of work for almost a year. Prior to that, I was the 'consultant to the consultants,' providing IT consulting to worldwide consultancies, but now I found myself taking a job with a mid-level accounting firm that also happened to provide IT consulting.

"I worked for a man who never got out from behind his desk, let alone left the office. He was completely clueless about technology, and a total idiot. In short, he was extremely unlikable. In fact, he was about to serve his wife with divorce papers but held off because she had been in a car accident. He wasn't waiting because he felt bad for her or wanted to help her with her rehabilitation. He was waiting so he wouldn't miss out on the personal injury settlement. He was repulsive.

"After five years of giving him ideas that made the business expand, he said he wanted to give me some help. He hired a complete buffoon to help pick up some of my workload. I found out the new guy was being paid as much as me. I figured this isn't my helper but probably my replacement. A week later I handed in my resignation and went to work for myself."

We are happy to report that Manny's IT consulting business, where he is basically doing what he did for his boss himself, is going well.

WHEN DO YOU QUIT?

"So far all you have been saying is start something! But I've been at it a long time with no success. How do I know when to stop?"
The simple answer is you stop when:

► You don't want to do it anymore. Either you are sick of what you are doing, or you can't figure out how to make money at it, if making money was your goal.

► You've proved to yourself that it can't be done (e.g., it's not technically feasible, there's no market at a workable price point, etc.) or you can't do it.

► You can't create a next step within your acceptable loss. (See our discussion in Chapter 4.)

Unfortunately, there are three practical problems with this recipe.

Let's take "I don't want to do this anymore" first. If you are sick of it, that's easy. You just quit. You don't need us to tell you that.

But suppose you still want to do it, but you can't make money at it. Keep at it—just keep at it *less*. That is, don't spend so much time on it. It becomes something you do on nights and weekends or maybe even as a hobby. If you like it, then keep at it, in whatever form you can. It just slips down—and perhaps slips down substantially—on the priority list of where you spend your time.

Proving it can't be done is more problematic. If you are trying to do something that's never been done before, you have no certainty about whether it (or you) could ultimately be successful with one more push, one more investment. Logicians proved a long time ago that you can't prove anything impossible. So when do you quit? If you can still act within your acceptable loss, you don't. You keep at it (unless, of course, the desire is gone).

But as you think about whether you can afford to continue, think about this as well: Are you still pursuing this idea because you want to, or are you doing it out of habit?

Let's try to shine a little light on this question. It has two parts.

You've been getting up every morning working on whatever it is you are doing and it has probably been a long time since you asked, "Why am I doing this?" By simply asking the question, you may realize that the desire is gone and it is time to move on to something else.

The pausing will get you to address something else. You always want to be standing on firm ground. You always want to know exactly where you are. So the ability to take stock of current reality is incredibly important.

You may have been doing whatever you're doing for so long that the world may have shifted around you. To use a silly example to make the point, you may have been laboring so long and so hard on perfecting your idea for a VCR that you fail to see that the world has moved on to digital recorders.

The way the world really is, is not necessarily the way you would like it to be. You might, indeed, be able to change the world. But to do that, you need to understand where the world is now. This can be an Achilles' heel for some. They can get so caught up in what they are trying to do that they fail to perceive current reality as clearly as they otherwise might.

Don't spend a lot of time thinking about this alone. Talk to your friends and colleagues. You need different perspectives. You need their help to see things differently, things you are missing.

REASON 5:
YOU KNOW YOU COULD DO IT BETTER

This common reason people give for starting a new business stems from their experience and knowledge of the field they work in. The more familiar they are with their company's operation, the more confident they become that they can do it themselves—and do it better.

People get frustrated because their employer is unwilling to take advantage of an opportunity they see, or they believe their employer is treating customers badly, and so they basically set off to replicate what their employer is doing, but on their own terms and with a higher level of quality.

As one reader wrote us in summing up succinctly what many people told us: "I knew I could do it better my way."

REASON 6:
JUST HAD TO DO IT

One of the most intriguing responses we got repeatedly, when we asked people to tell us why they started their business, was that they were personally compelled to do so.

It wasn't that they saw a niche in the marketplace they had to fill. It was because they had to do something creative/challenging/fulfilling/satisfying on their own. They just couldn't imagine, as Kaitki Agarwal told us, spending the rest of their life on the mundane. Says Agarwal, "I started my own company because I like to innovate, do something challenging and different, something that will cause disruption, make people's life better. I am not the kind of person who likes doing regular work; I need to do something new and interesting every day. The corporate world is too restricting. I have to be in charge of my working life."

Rozbeh Nassab tells a similar story:

"I was working as a freelance web developer and my friend, Myuran Balendran, was a software developer in the investment banking industry. Neither of us felt challenged by our work and both of us wanted to push ourselves further. We felt the day-to-day tasks involved with our jobs were not enough to keep us content on a long-term basis.

"Rolio, the company we started, solves a real-life problem. With the constant growth of the Internet and the sheer number of websites available online, keeping track of the content that most interests you has never been more difficult. Rolio aggregates real-time content from your favorite websites, including Facebook and Twitter, into one visual interface that not only saves you a lot of time, it also eliminates the need for you to have multiple browser windows open at the same time.

"Although other RSS readers are available, Rolio is not like other typical RSS readers. The other readers are dull and don't cater to the nontechnical user like Rolio does. We have taken a more visual approach which also integrates social media and includes an interactive interface."

REASON 7:
NECESSITY-BASED ENTREPRENEURSHIP

Related to the necessity argument is one that is near and dear to my heart. *You got fired.* Let me share my story, before sharing what you told us.

Here goes. John F. Kennedy said he became a war hero because "they sank my boat." I became an entrepreneur because I got thrown out of my job.

The background is simple. It was a Thursday in 1993, and I was about to stand up to the man who owned our publishing company. He had just issued an order that cut the legs out from under my boss, the man who ran the editorial side of the magazine I worked for.

Since I a) liked my boss, b) thought it was a truly bad decision, c) would be the person who would have to make the lousy decision work (I was managing editor), and d) was raised to speak directly to people with whom you disagree (instead of complaining behind their backs), I felt compelled to say something.

I went to our owner and said, "Look, I understand what you want to do, and it is your candy store. If you really want to do this, I promise I will execute it to the absolute best of my ability, but it is a truly bad idea for the following reasons," and I went on for two or three minutes explaining the potential problems in detail. There really were a lot of them.

The owner thanked me for my "honesty and candor" and for having the "guts" to confront him. "I like that in an employee," he told me. "I am still going to do what I want to do, but I am giving you a $15,000 raise effective immediately." I went home Thursday night feeling pretty good about myself.

Friday morning, I was summoned to the owner's office. "Paul, I've thought a lot about our conversation yesterday. You're fired. You can leave right now. There is no reason to go back to your office. We will have someone pack up your stuff and ship it to you."

I had a stay-at-home wife, two kids (ages 6 and 11), and lived in a very nice Manhattan suburb in a house that came complete with a mortgage that would, as my grandmother used to say, "choke a horse."

I'd like to tell you that at that moment I said to myself, "This is the perfect time to start a company." But I didn't. I was a "magazine guy." All I ever wanted to do from the time I was in college was work at a national magazine, and so I spent the next couple months frantically trying to land a new gig. But even then, publishing as an industry was shrinking, and while people offered me all kinds of elaborate contract arrangements, nobody presented me with a full-time job offer. And so, kicking and screaming, I became an entrepreneur.

It turns out that my story is far from unique. As Zanade Mann wrote in to our website, "They fired my whole department in 2009. I took my severance pay and created several opportunities for myself."

OKAY, I NEED TO BE AN ENTREPRENEUR. WHAT'S IT GOING TO COST?

How much money do you need to start your own company?

As the Kauffman Foundation, the world's largest institution devoted to entrepreneurship, notes correctly in a study, "The answer, of course, depends on what kind of company you are creating." If you are starting a biotech firm or a company that makes earth-moving equipment, you are likely to require millions, for example. If you are going to paint pictures for a living or start a transcription business, the cost is virtually zero.

That's true, but not particularly helpful. So, fortunately, the foundation went a bit further to shed some light on the subject. It tracked 4,928 firms launched in 2004 and found that the average cost was $109,016. The figure was $44,793 for firms without employees and $58,448 for home-based firms.

Those numbers are not chicken feed—unless you have an amazing number of chickens—but are probably not hopelessly daunting for most people.

Where does the money come from? Surprisingly, the biggest source is bank loans (35 percent). Personal funds came second, at 30 percent. So, those two sources made up about two-thirds of the total on average. "Friends and families help," providing about 6 percent of total funding. Another personal source, using credit cards, provides 6 percent. Together, venture capital funding, angel investors, and government money made up less than 12 percent with the rest of the funds coming from other sources, according to the research.

Yes, of course, these are average figures, and your experience could be different. But there are a couple of things that seem clear from the data. First, while it is truly a dumb idea to use credit cards as a source of start-up funding, given the ridiculously high interest rates the credit card companies charge, people still do it. And it also seems clear, as the study says, that "you should not start planning your business around funding sources like VCs, angels, and government funding. They simply do not appear to be significant sources in most cases."

REASON 8:
THIS IS HOW I WANT TO SPEND MY TIME

What surprises some people is the next reason for starting a business: for the lifestyle. Listen to Lance:

"I dropped out of college and didn't finish my degree. So there it began. I would work this job and not like it for some reason. I would work that job and not like it for a different reason. It went on and on. I wanted to work for a business that was honest and upfront and truly wanted to help people, but I never seemed to be able to find a fit.

"One thing I always wanted in a job or career was flexibility. My dad always told me there are two ways to make money and have flexibility in this world: 'Be in sales or start your own business.' So I tried sales! Loved it at first, but quickly found out that I was still working for someone and it wasn't quite all I had hoped for. So I took a very considerable pay cut and took another sales job that allowed me to start a business. I knew that if I didn't want to answer to anyone but myself, this was the only option. Instead of trying a different [job] and getting the same outcome, I created my own method! I am working hard every day to make a success of the business I started and I am loving every minute of it!"

For some people, it simply was time to go off on their own. This comment comes from someone who self-identifies as a "Mktg Science Group" as he (or she) responded to a post on the Action Trumps Everything blog (http://www.forbes.com/sites/actiontrumpseverything/): "After working in various marketing roles, I began to get disenchanted with the lack of innovation in the profession. If you talk to most agencies, their fundamental business model is the same as it's been since the 1960s.

"When a company I had been with at senior management level for less than a year was purchased by a larger company with very conservative values, I started the usual job search. After a few months of disappointing conversations with a variety of business owners about marketing roles, I figured the smartest thing for me to do was strike out on my own with a fresh take on the marketing agency business model.

"I felt like the tumblers on the 'career slot machine' had lined up and I needed to pull the lever: timing (a down economy is a great time to start a business), market opportunity (marketing agencies have become stale and aren't adopting new tools and business models fast enough), and personal situation (twenty years' experience with a great network, an understanding of what it would take, stable finances, etc.)."

REASON 9:
THE LIGHTBULB FINALLY WENT ON

For others we talked to, they just keep zigging and zagging until something clicked.

Lukeither Willingham begins:

"Starting my own company is a work in progress and was not my original plan. I began my company as a backup plan to a plan that backfired and to survive the recession, but it has brought me some wonderful successes and some embarrassing failures.

"My successes include being at home during my daughter's formative growing stages, helping other entrepreneurs make the transition, and having some impressive clients; but failures have included making some shortsighted decisions, and revenue hasn't been steady or consistent, but I've dealt with that by using that slow time to continue to learn as much as I can and stay current with changes in my industry, and it's working.

"Being an early adapter to social media and being online has enabled me to stay involved in my industry, stay visible, and identify when to make changes with my products and services. I've been able to make great connections and I've caught a few fish with this strategy, but I am still fishing to catch that whale."

"I FIGURED I HAD AS GOOD A SHOT
AS ANYONE"

Billy Sorenson was a sophomore at Utah Valley University and happened to be watching *The Tonight Show with Jay Leno* on a night when billionaire oil man T. Boone Pickens was a guest. Pickens was promoting his book *The First Billion Is the Hardest: Reflections on a Life of Comebacks and America's Energy Future.*

Sorenson was intrigued by Pickens and went out and bought the book.

Pickens's argument was that the next great "oil boom" was going to be in wind and solar, and he was betting a huge part of his fortune on wind.

"I figured if he had wind sewn up, I could do solar," Sorenson, then age 20, recalled.

What did he know about the energy business? Not a thing. He was in the university's entrepreneurship program as preparation to take over the family photography business. But the way Sorenson saw it, that lack of knowledge wasn't a liability. Nobody knew very much about alternative energy back then. "It didn't strike me as weird. It was a new industry. I figured I would have as good a shot as anyone."

He talked the idea over with his good friend David Richards and RS Energy was born. Says Sorenson, "One of the things Pickens's book talked about was all the tax credits that were going to be available to companies and consumers who sold or installed alternative energy, so David's background— he was a junior majoring in accounting—was perfect."

The question was where to begin. Industry knowledge struck both young men as a good idea, and so they started attending trade shows. "I think the first question I asked someone was what a watt was," Sorenson recalled.

But they were quick studies and soon discovered what they thought was a huge opportunity. Clearly, universities would want to be on the cutting edge of powering their campuses with alternative energy. "So we set up meetings with the universities in Utah, put on our suits, and started talking to various officials."

The good news? The schools were indeed interested. The bad news? RS Energy would need about $8 million in capital to make the first project happen. There was no way they could raise that kind of money.

What other opportunities were there? Well, at the other end of the spectrum, homeowners, too, were interested in alternative energy, and Sorenson heard of various programs to do residential retrofits in Portland, Oregon.

"Switching gears wasn't all that hard," Sorenson says. After all, when you don't have much you don't have much to lose.

Doing one house at a time, the company generated revenues of $350,000 in 2009 and the business was underway. Their work drew the attention of people in other parts of the city, and RS Energy became an integral part of the 2010 "Solarize Portland" campaign that local officials were running. That in turn got them to various residential construction firms that wanted to offer solar energy as part of their developments, and from there to agricultural work for farmers looking to lower their energy costs. In 2011, revenues came in at $4.7 million and the future looks bright. "We now have eighteen employees and should do at least $7 million in business with a gross profit margin of about 28 percent," Sorenson says.

The point of telling these stories is fourfold:

First, they're representative of the literally tens of thousands of people who started acting like entrepreneurs in their quest to navigate the uncertain economy we all now operate in.

Second, you can see that there is neither one overarching reason that gets people to act, nor is there one route from getting from here to there. While the process is the same (Act. Learn. Build. Repeat.), the particular paths people choose are always different.

Third, as you just read in these stories, that path will probably be far from straight. And you might end up in a place you never anticipated.

Fourth, the people who have taken the plunge say they are happy. There were often bumps, disappointments, or even setbacks to deal with, but not one of them expressed any longing to go back to a corporate job. That's a good thing. Because traditional corporate jobs are disappearing and are not coming back.

WHAT DO YOU DO WHEN
YOU DON'T HAVE AN IDEA?

Okay, you concede, everyone has to be an entrepreneur or at least develop entrepreneurial-type thinking and action. But what the heck do you do if you haven't an idea for what you want to create in order to put those skills to work? What if you can't come up with an idea to get yourself started? What do you do?

Well, the place most people begin is by asking, "What am I good at?" And they go from there, figuring they will either start a company that capitalizes on their strengths; they will work as a consultant to someone who needs those skills; or they will eventually be hired full-time by a corporation that needs their expertise.

It's certainly an adequate place to start . . . but probably not the best.

Knowing who you are, whom you know, and what resources you have—your "current reality," to reduce all that to a single phrase—is a very good thing. However, the very best first step is to instead ask, "What do I actually care about?"

It's pretty obvious, actually. Desire, as we have seen, motivates you to act. It makes you persist when you encounter obstacles. And it makes you more creative, as we saw in Chapter 4. The net takeaway: Desire makes it more likely that you will create an idea.

You always know what you care about. Always. And it's rarely couched within the specifications of a specific job. (We have yet to meet anyone who has said, "I want to do statistical analysis of receivables for a Fortune 100 company.") Similarly, it is uncommon that the answer describes perfectly the company you end up starting or the job you end up taking. (As we have seen, your idea will inevitably evolve once you get underway.) But, if you honestly reflect, you will always have an answer to what's important to you. For example, you might say: "My favorite thing in the world is playing with numbers to solve or understand something."

Your desires will break down into two types. There are those things that we can call "Ultimate" Desires—things you want simply because you want them. They can range in intensity from those things you're just interested in ("It would be really cool if . . .") to those you would die for. But the defining characteristic is that you actually care about "it." You hear yourself saying, "I have to be an abstract painter (or architect, or engineer, or doctor, or worker in the local women's shelter) or I am going to be absolutely miserable."

When you have an Ultimate Desire, guess what? You already have an idea. ("My favorite thing in the world is playing with numbers to solve or understand something.") What you're actually searching for is *how to do it*. What you are looking for is an acceptably low-cost next step, within your means at hand, to make it a reality. So don't get confused. Don't say you don't have an idea. You do. ("I want to play with numbers.") You just haven't developed the next step. ("I am not sure yet what the job that will allow me to do that looks like.") The thing you most need to do at this point is figure out how to get moving.

The second kind of desire is when you want something because you think it will bring you something else. Here's an easy example: "I really like the idea of starting my own firm, not because I want to run a company, but because I think that's going to provide me with gainful employment." (Or make me famous, à la Mark Zuckerberg, or ensure that I never have to work for anyone else again in my life.) The specific thing isn't what you want so much as what you think it's going to lead you to. Think of these things as "Instrumental" Desires, things that you want because they lead to an Ultimate Desire. These are the cases in which you need an idea.

How do you obtain one? Thinking, analysis, and introspection aren't bad—they could trigger an idea—but you also want to be acting as soon as you can. You want to be doing something. If that thinking, analysis, and introspection slows down your acting, it's not so good. What you get, over and over, are people sitting around the kitchen table night after night and month after month and year after year trying to think up an idea but never doing anything.

The reality, when you dig a little deeper, is that they had *lots* of ideas: "maybe I'll open a restaurant; maybe a personal shopper service; maybe. . . ." So why did nothing happen? They either didn't think any of those ideas were good enough, or they were spending all that time at the kitchen table trying to refine them (on paper), or they are spending all their time playing "what if" games (solely in their head) pondering tens or hundreds of scenarios that might or might not happen. They would have been far better off getting out and doing something because—as we have seen—action changes reality and thinking *doesn't*.

After every action you have new opportunities, potentially new partners, and fresh ideas. If you are sitting around your kitchen table and not acting, nothing happens.

How could this acting your way into a solution work? Well, do you like to cook? Whip up six different versions of the same recipe and hold a blind tasting at the church bazaar. Could you do something with the one recipe that everyone loves?

See a problem that no one has solved? Sketch out a solution and talk it through with people who have the problem. As a result, maybe your "personal shopper service" morphs into a high-end house-sitting business. Perhaps your restaurant idea turns into an idea for providing frozen, ready-to-eat meals for people with severe dietary restrictions.

Sure, ideas can arise in a flash of insight. But more often (and more reliably) your Ultimate Desire will surface and your idea will develop through your interactions with other people or the marketplace. You don't need the idea as much as you need to get started. Worst case? You take a few tiny steps and discover you don't like what you're doing. Or it's impossible. If that happens, you reboot and move on to something else.

ONE OTHER THOUGHT

None of these ideas appeal to you? Here's an approach that is being developed by one of the participants in Charles Kiefer's Just Start course (Just-Start.com). Tom McDonough calls it "twelve weeks to having entrepreneurial skills."

Tom starts with the premise that there are only two kinds

of business: those that are knowledge-based and those that revolve around manufacturing. He follows that with two other thoughts that we also agree with:

1. Everyone is expert in something. Can you construct some sort of way of getting paid for it? For example, you could use Udemy.com and create a course that people will pay for.

2. If your business idea revolves around manufacturing, could you make something and sell it on eBay?

How would that work?

It is not as hard as you think. Tom suggests that to remain motivated, you do this with a few friends who mutually commit to supporting each other. Each person:

a) Determines an acceptable hourly wage for him/herself.

b) Commits to creating a business that at the end of twelve weeks:

  ► Runs on a couple hours of effort.

  ► Yields profit equal to or exceeding the acceptable hourly wage.

  ► Can be shut down easily.

And you get underway. At the end of twelve weeks, you will have proven that you can get a company up and running and can sell a product. You could discover that whatever you have decided to produce is something that you really like to do. At the very least, you will know that you can take action and produce positive results.

A DIFFERENT LENS FOR LOOKING AT THE CURRENT REALITY

When it comes to generating ideas, are Ultimate Desires better than Instrumental ones? No. Are Instrumental ones better than Ultimate ones? No again. They both can lead you to a Big Idea. But knowing which is which is very important, because they each take you down different roads.

In the case of the Ultimate Desire, you are going to pursue it because you have to. If you don't have the skills right now, you will develop them along the way. If you don't have the contacts or network right now, you will develop them along the way, too.

Here's a quick example. A woman we know has a passion for kids in the juvenile justice system. She was looking around to find something she could do to help them. Her Ultimate Desire was clear. She wanted to work with those kids and make their lives better. It was the kind of thing she would do, even if she never made a dime.

So she got started with what she had at hand, which wasn't much: a tiny storefront and a bunch of books people donated. She opened a used bookstore and got at-risk kids to sell the books in the store and online. She has been remarkably successful in keeping these troubled kids from going back into the juvenile justice system.

Did she know a thing about books or retail or even that much about how to deal with troubled youth before she began? No. But her desire was so strong that none of that mattered much.

Now, let's take a look at Instrumental Desire, the desire that leads to something you truly want. You're looking around for an idea because you think it's going to bring you employment or because you think it will bring you, for the sake of illustration, fame or fortune. So, you know the answer to the question "What do I want?" You want the fame. You want the employment. You want the money. Whatever end goal you have is valid. But since the immediate goal (the thing you are starting) is a means to an end ("I am founding a company to become rich"), knowing your skills, interests, assets, and the rest is really important because you want to do something you like, in an area where you excel, because it will be easier than starting completely from scratch with no particular background or skills.

But be careful! When you start with certain questions—What am I good at? Who do I know? What do I know? What resources do I have at hand? What can I do with all those things?—you may begin to go down the path of figuring out what you can do with those resources. That in and of itself is not wrong, but what often gets lost in the shuffle is what you actually want: that is, your ultimate goal of fame, money, or whatever. You could end up pursuing something that makes a lot of sense (because you're a terrific baker) but that you don't actually care about (because baking bores you to tears). If that happens, it will be difficult for you to maintain your focus. You'll have to flog yourself to get into action, and you probably won't be as creative as you might otherwise be.

The better plan, once you know what your ultimate aim is, is to take a reasonably thorough but quick inventory of current reality—you are terrific with figures—find something intrinsically attractive—"you know handling the finances of a new nonprofit that does X could be really interesting"—and get started. Learn along the way.

You'll have an idea. See if it is the right one.

WHAT WE JUST COVERED— *AND WHAT'S AHEAD*

1. Being thrown out of work is only one of the nine reasons people start companies.

2. Some people always knew they would start a company of their own. Others came to the concept of entrepreneurship kicking and screaming.

3. While the motivations to start a company were different, many people have used the same Act. Learn. Build. Repeat. model that we have discussed throughout.

In the next chapter, we'll explore how you can practice the ALBR model and make yourself happier in the process.

You Don't Have to Be an Entrepreneur

(How to Think and Act Entrepreneurially *Without* Starting a Business)

CHAPTER 8

Practice Outside of Work

Not ready to take the entrepreneurial plunge? Not yet convinced that your job is going to go away? Fine. Still, it never hurts to be prepared. Here are two ways to go about it.

Let's say you are willing to meet us halfway. You'll concede your job may go away. But you are not quite ready to go full bore to prepare for what that means.

We understand. Change can be scary, and if a threat isn't imminent—for example, no one has told you your job will be eliminated in four months—it can be difficult to change.

Fine.

So, let's look at the situation differently. Are you absolutely thrilled with the way things are going at your current job? If not, what we are about to propose could help you lay the foundation for the next phase of your life. You'll see that we aren't arguing that you need to start a new company tomorrow. But we are advocating that you learn how to master entrepreneurial thought and action so that you are able to succeed in whatever you do next.

And even if you are happy, if you follow our advice, you just might end up being even happier. That is no small thing.

It would be nice to think you are going to be just as excited about going to the office tomorrow as you were on your first day on the job. But between increased workloads caused by your company's reluctance to hire more people, and possibly a change in management that has put less than stellar people in charge of your corner of the universe—and maybe because you have done the same job for a while now—you may be feeling . . . well, not exactly burned out, but fatigued.

What's a person to do?

➤ Telling yourself to get more excited about the same old thing isn't going to work. (It never does.) All the psychological tricks you have probably heard—challenge yourself every day; think of all the things you have accomplished; be grateful you have a job—can work for a while, but they are not long-term solutions.

➤ Retiring in place and simply going through the motions is not an option. You'd be replaced a week from Thursday by someone who might not be better, but who will certainly have more enthusiasm. And these days you would be hard pressed to find a company, or any organization anywhere for that matter, that is letting anyone collect a paycheck for doing very little.

➤ Looking for another job is clearly a choice, but terrific jobs are hard to come by in this limp-along economy, and if we are right about the workplace being permanently upended, that could be a temporary solution at best. That new job you find could disappear just as fast as your current one.

Let us suggest another alternative: Start something. More specifically, start something outside of work.

It could be a new company, or at least something that could lead you to starting your own company. (It begins as a part-time business, perhaps.) But it also could be something artsy (writing a book, composing songs) or doing something for the betterment of your community (promoting an idea for a new after-school program or getting bicycle paths installed in town). Heck, it could even be something you have always wanted to do, an activity that probably has no financial reward (learning the piano, speaking a new language, or mastering juggling).

It doesn't matter what it is. The key is to start—as in, take a small step toward what you think you want, as we talked about before. You don't have to make a commitment to see this fledging notion through to the end. (That would be silly; you simply don't know if this new thing is something that you are going to like, be good at, or if you will be able to complete it given everything else going on in your life.) The key is to get moving without much cost, either in time, money, or any other resource.

As with all new ventures—business or otherwise—you want to stay within your acceptable loss. (See our discussion in Chapter 4.) You never want to risk more than you can afford to lose.

Once you take that small (inexpensive) step, stop to examine what you have learned. If you are happy with the results, take another step toward your goal. Then pause to see what you have learned from taking that second step, and if it feels right, go take another. (As you can see the process here is exactly the same as we outlined previously.)

How is this going to make you happier at your day job? That's simple. Some of the enthusiasm you have for your outside venture is going to carry over into the office. Making progress on things you care about elevates your mood. And since you take your mind with you everywhere you go, you will take your improved mood with you as well. You'll come to work pleased with yourself ("Hey, I've mastered

'Mary Had a Little Lamb' on the piano using all ten fingers") and you will be less dour. Guaranteed. That could be enough to get you out of your funk, which is certainly a good thing for you, your colleagues, and your company.

And if it doesn't cure your day job fatigue, or it doesn't for long, that is not necessarily bad, either. By taking the step toward creating something outside of work, you have done two things, both of them good.

First, you may have started down the road that could lead to you starting your own business. (Selling those birdhouses that you build, the ones everyone raves about, actually shows signs of turning into a small company. See the sidebar "Where Are You?")

WHERE ARE YOU?

Brandon Medenwald, 29, is the classic example of what we are talking about here.

"I'm the co-founder of Simply Made Apps, a three-person start-up based in Fargo, North Dakota that develops software for the web, iPhone, and Android platforms. Currently our sole app is Simple In/Out (simpleinout.com), a digital in/out board for offices.

"Our start-up story is a classic example of scratching your own itch. I personally had problems with our in/out software at my day job (as a software developer for a firm that serves the real estate industry). It was always out of date because people would forget to use it. I would joke that 'I could write a better solution in a weekend.'

"After chewing on this boast for a while, I had an epiphany: to use a cell phone's GPS to solve the problem. Most cell phones have a GPS feature and you could use it to let people know where you were. Your cell phone would provide the location. I pitched the idea to a couple of my friends over beers and Simple In/Out's core innovation was born.

"We each threw in a little start-up money [a *total* of less than $500] to cover expenses, and the rest is history," he says. "We all still have day jobs that pay the bills, but our little business is where our passion for making something truly outstanding gets to shine."

Could this endeavor grow into a real company that provides him full-time employment? It could. Medenwald and his two friends have ideas for other simple ideas they think they would like to develop. At the moment, revenues are small and just provide "beer money," but the company is profitable and producing enough in sales to develop a marketing budget.

"We are focused on the goal of providing simple applications that can help people and companies," Medenwald says. "But we don't have to chase money and do things that take us away from that, because we all have jobs. We can take our time."

Second, because you have done it, you have proven to yourself that you know how to create something new. (You have gotten Birdhouses R Us up and running and generating a tiny profit; your idea to have your town install bike paths has become a reality and people are bicycling more safely.) Knowing how to create something new, as we have argued throughout, will be a valuable skill to have no matter what you do next, be it starting your own company, looking for another traditional job, or trying to carve out a new sort of position that will make you happier.

Of course, there is an alternative, and you probably have met the person who has taken it. He's the guy who tells you about all the things he might do—that might be exciting to him—but who never seems to take step one. You offer encouragement and support. You even suggest a couple of variations on what he is talking about that could get him going faster. But nothing happens. The only response you get from him is, "I will get around to it someday."

Somehow he seems more comfortable—and, ironically, even pleased—with dreaming about possibilities than actually doing anything about them.

The remedy for this malaise is simple (though not often taken). It is the first step in the ALBR model. It is to act. Every action causes a change in reality. Every action carries the potential for learning. Learning about your next step. Learning about what you like or don't like. Learning what gets a positive reaction in the marketplace, and what doesn't.

Every act can build momentum. Small desires grow. A small talent or expertise can be developed and honed. Before you know it, you can be on a new course. But only if you act.

So, as counterintuitive as it seems, to be more excited about your day job, you may want to moonlight.

SIMPLE, BUT NOT EASY

If you are going to try to navigate this tricky path, you must:

➤ (Continue to) do excellent work at your day job.

➤ Not moonlight on company time.

➤ Not spend a lot of (and perhaps no) time talking about your outside activities to people you work with.

If you adhere to these recommendations, is treading water for a while at your job—while you cultivate your outside interest—an awful idea?

Not really.

For one thing, it is possible, as we said, that the enthusiasm from your outside activities could make you more energized at work. (All those orders for Birdhouses R Us have you fired up and you are transferring that renewed energy into your day job.) But, even if it doesn't, offering a solid day's work for a day's pay is going to strike your employer as a fair deal—at least for a while (remember, the expectation is that you are going to continue to do a good job at work)—and collecting a steady paycheck isn't the worst thing.

But at some point, if your lack of enthusiasm is apparent, your boss is going to replace you with someone who truly wants to do what you are doing. Hopefully, that won't happen immediately.

IS IT CHEATING TO HAVE A SIDE PROJECT?

The obvious question about all this is: Are you cheating your boss by working on something else outside of work? One manager we put the question to didn't hesitate for a second before he answered "yes": "When people get excited about things outside of work, they end up showing up to work and going through motions just to get through a day. Maybe they don't mean to do it, but they do. As a result, everyone loses. The employee loses and the employer loses. People are not going to give all of themselves as they focus on their new outside interest."

He makes an extremely valid point, one that is worth exploring.

Everything we have recommended—starting something new beyond your job; putting in an hour a day to learn a new skill/profession (see Chapter 3)—needs to be *outside* of office hours. If you do it on company time you can be fired, and quite frankly, you should be.

If you are a PR guy who is in your office behind closed doors working on your stand-up routines instead of figuring out ways to advance the interests of your clients, you deserve to lose your job. If you are an operating systems software engineer who spends even part of the time you are on the clock working on your great idea for a new video game, you should be collecting unemployment.

If your passion for creating something new is *that* all encompassing, then quit and go pursue it. It is the only honest thing to do.

Here's why. You entered into a contract (written or implied) with the company that employs you. They promised to pay you in exchange for your time or the results of your creativity. If you are working on something else, on company time, you are not fulfilling your end of the bargain. You are stealing. It's that simple.

Ah, you say. I am in a creative profession and creativity does not occur only between nine and five, and solely in the office. What difference does it make if I use breaks during the day—or when I am stuck—to think about an outside gig, as long as I get my work done?

It's a great question. And the answer is: It matters a lot.

If—and it is a big if—you can manage that, then great. But you darn well better make sure that you are delivering more than 100 percent of what you promised the boss. The more you deliver above and beyond what your "contract" calls for, the more slack you will get. If you are only doing an adequate or marginal job—or even a good one—you are painting a very large target on your back and inviting people—colleagues, your boss, your boss's boss—to take shots at you.

Yes, you should be preparing yourself for the next job, but you better be doing it on your own time (unless your company has put you in a specific training program to prepare you for the next promotion or assignment). If you're unfulfilled at work, then we say that you should find something fulfilling outside of it. And we mean exactly that. Outside of it. It is in addition to your day job, not instead of it.

But all that said, you do owe it to yourself to keep other irons in the fire. Your company no longer has a commitment to lifelong employment. Sad as it is, the operative contract today is that the company will discard you as soon as the economic forces tilt in that direction. Or those forces make your company and, conceivably, your industry, irrelevant. Be a good Boy Scout—be prepared! It's the only responsible thing to do for you and your loved ones.

Now you may believe with good reason that the company expects 100 percent of your time, and that you won't be promoted if you don't deliver unending hours (which might mean responding to emails while on your rare vacations, holding international calls at two in the morning, or finishing reports on nights and weekends). You may well be right.

Our point is not that you shouldn't meet these demanding demands. It's a judgment call on your part; if you think it is the only way to keep your job, so be it. But if you are committing your all in this fashion, then you need to be extremely certain that you are building transferable expertise. And transferable, ideally, to an entirely different industry, just in case yours ends up disappearing.

The parents of Baby Boomers believed (correctly for the most part, as it turned out) that the trajectory of their careers would be continuously higher: They would obtain positions of increasing responsibility as they stayed perhaps with one company their entire lives. We Baby Boomers left college with this thought pretty well established in our minds. And while some of us were disrupted, many of us—especially the older boomers—made it to the finish line of a pension-based retirement.

Kids today don't even consider this a remote possibility. They assume a life with career disruptions, even if they don't describe it in these terms.

What about the folks in their thirties and forties? Odds are you will have to reinvent yourself at least once during your working life, and maybe twice. This doesn't mean you'll have to change a little. It may well mean a change of career.

It may not happen to you—but what if it does? Are you prepared?

WHAT WE JUST COVERED—
AND WHAT'S AHEAD

1. If you want to be more excited about your day job, do something outside of it. The enthusiasm you have for what you do outside of work is going stay with you when you are back at the office.

2. If it doesn't make you more excited about work . . . you still have accomplished two things. You have started something that may lead you to your next job or career. And you will have proven to yourself that you have the ability to start something new.

3. It is not cheating to have a side project—provided you really only work on it outside of work and that your performance at your day job remains high.

In the next chapter we will discuss how to apply the ALBR approach to three common career situations.

CHAPTER 9

Using the
Act. Learn. Build. Repeat. (ALBR)
Model to Find a Job

The approach that allows you to start your own company also works if you would prefer to be employed by someone else.

Sure, as we discussed, you can use the ALBR model to

start a company, a move that would provide employment for you in the process.

But using ALBR is equally effective if you want to find a new job, are entering the workforce for the first time, or are rejoining it after a prolonged absence whether by choice (e.g., you took some time out for child-rearing or military service) or not (e.g., a chronic condition kept you from working, or you were one of the many millions who became a victim of the Great Recession).

How would this work? Let's begin with using ALBR to look for a new job.

JOB HUNTING

You know what the classic job hunt looks like, of course. The presumption is that it is like a game of "hide and seek": The right job is out there, if only you can find it. Maybe you take various tests (like the aptitude tests you took in high school) to see what jobs are a good match—or maybe you don't. In either case, you are told to network, network, network, and network some more.

And so, that's what people do. They call up every person they can think of, and every name that they have been able to get from friends, friends of friends, friends of friends of friends, colleagues, or whoever, and ask for informational interviews. And at the end of those conversations they ask for even more names of people they can talk to.

It's a great approach, but if you do only that, it will be limiting. It assumes, as we said, that there is a job out there and all you have to do is *find* it.

But suppose on top of looking for a new job in the traditional way, you also set off to *create* a job within a company you would like to work for. What would that look like? How might that work?

You are going to act, of course. But before you do, you need to figure out what you want to happen. In other words, you'd begin with what you want, what you desire.

DESIRE

People often get into trouble right off the bat. They may begin by asking, "What am I good at?" On the surface, that seems fine, but as you dig a little deeper you see the problem. "I am the world's greatest desktop publisher" may be a true statement, but that fact really doesn't do you much good these days when just about everything has moved to the Internet. Neither does the fact that you are "a terrific cook," if the idea of cooking for a living bores you to tears.

Or they begin—as they should—by asking themselves what it is they *want* to do. But they end up defining the answer too narrowly and remain relentlessly focused on that small niche and/or on what they have always done for work.

It would be like asking a nine-year-old boy what he wants to be when he grows up and he says: "I am going to be the starting third baseman for the New York Yankees." That specificity, while appealing, is limiting. There is only one such position in the world and that is all there will ever be.

The same is often true for grown-ups. The answer to the question of what kind of job you are looking for could be very specific. For example, someone who is currently working in the research department of a business-to-business products company might say: "I want to be a researcher for one of the world's three biggest consumer packaged goods companies."* Obviously, research positions would exist within the three largest CPG companies. But equally obviously, there are only a limited number of them.

Our suggestion? Once you answer the what-kind-of-job-are-you-looking-for question, start asking yourself why you responded that way. It may be that you have fantasized about doing consumer research since you were a small child. But it is more likely that you want to be involved with a consumer products company, specifically

---

* As you may know, CPGs are things used by people (the consumer) every day. They include food, beverages, paper towels, toothpaste, and the like. They are items that are typically sold through supermarkets and grocery stores and that are used up and replaced often, as opposed to purchases like furniture and appliances, which last a long time.

in the research department, because you are intrigued by how people think, or you want to be able to draw a straight line between what you do and the new products that are created, or you like the idea of spending all day helping to figure out how to differentiate Brand X from Brand Y, or . . . .

The more you understand your motivation, the more likely it is that your insight will open up more potential career options. Let's say our would-be researcher's motivation was simply that he wanted to be involved in the consumer products industry. He wanted to feel truly connected to what is going on in the economy when he reads the business section of the paper every morning, and he loves the idea of understanding why certain goods are stocked at Wal-Mart, Target, Macy's, and his local supermarket.

That realization could lead him to look for work beyond the research department of one of the top CPG firms. Relatively easily he could shift over into the marketing department of just about any firm that sells to the consumer. Or he could take his research skills in a different direction and use them at a brokerage firm on Wall Street, recommending whether someone should buy one publicly held consumer goods company over another.

ACT

You can see how understanding desire affects the first step in the ALBR model: taking action. Let's stay with our researcher example. Knowing now that his fundamental desire is to be part of the consumer packaged goods industry broadly defined, obviously he is going to be networking for positions beyond what he first thought. Yes, of course he is going to be looking for research positions within the top-three CPG companies, but he is also going to expand his search. He will be looking, if he is smart, at every large CPG company. P & G, probably the largest CPG, has sales well north of $80 billion a year. Simply broadening his search to companies with "just" $1 billion in revenue will open up another forty-nine places to apply, according to Hunt Executive Search, which keeps track of this sort of thing.

YOU ARE ONLY ONE INSIGHT AWAY FROM BEING AS RICH AS WARREN BUFFETT, BILL GATES, OR OPRAH

On one level, of course, the headline is obvious. The insight that leads you to cure the common cold, or create that perpetual motion machine, should make you extremely wealthy.

However, the headline also makes a point that is often overlooked. The more insights you have, the greater your chances of overall success.

But that isn't the way many of us look at it.

Think back to the hype surrounding Facebook going public. Before its initial public offering (IPO), owners of small businesses and start-ups—and investors in general—were focused on the billions of dollars that company founder Mark Zuckerberg would make the moment his firm went public. It was easy to conclude that getting venture capital funding, as Zuckerberg did, was the way to go, if you wanted to have success.

To follow the route he took, you'd plan for what would

feel like forever. You'd assemble a team, which would take more time. And then you'd network like crazy to get to a venture capitalist who would meet with you.

If the VC finally did see you, it could take as long as two years to get the money you need—and that's only if the venture capital firm decided to fund you, which it likely wouldn't. Venture capitalists back about 1,200 out of the 600,000 new businesses started every year. Of those 600,000, the Small Business Administration says 66 percent survive two years.

If you do the math, you'll find that in that same two-year period, you might start and fail in two ventures and have begun a third, all by bootstrapping and tapping family and friends. The odds favor one of those ventures working, leaving you with a good chance of owning a successful firm. In contrast, with venture capitalist funding, your firm would have just a 0.2 percent chance of surviving more than two years. That means there is a *huge* chance you would have absolutely nothing to show for several years of effort.

The point here is simple: the more insights the better. And the more quickly you discover if there is a market for what you want to do, the better still.

Ironically, it turns out that if you want to be as rich as Mark Zuckerberg, you probably don't want to take the route he did. Rather, you want to test your idea as soon as possible—don't wait until it's perfect—and see how the market reacts. If it looks like it isn't going to work, you can quickly move on to something else (and then you haven't wasted a whole lot of time or money).

That way you will have plenty of resources left to try to develop an insight that will make you as rich as Warren Buffett, Bill Gates, or Oprah.

And, if the researcher really wants to be effective, he won't sit back passively waiting for all those résumés he sent out and all the phone calls and interviews he has done to pay off. He will be taking not only classes that update his current skills, but also courses that could expand them. For example, he might start working on an MBA with a marketing concentration.

LEARN/BUILD

Based on the reaction to his small steps toward finding another job, our would-be researcher discovers that moving beyond what he has always done is going to be harder than he thought. Yes, people understand that his skills in analyzing what businesses or consumers are likely to buy are transferable to other areas, such as finance, but they are concerned that there is no proof he would be good working in those new areas. After all, he has never done it.

So he recognizes that concern, and makes a conscious decision to eliminate it by:

1. Getting his MBA as quickly as possible.

2. Joining associations that deal with more than just research.

3. Going back and reworking how he has been presenting his background in order to highlight the gains his research insights have generated for his employers. He changes his résumé and how he presents himself at interviews as a result, broadening his appeal to potential employers.

4. Reviewing his network in a different light. For example, he begins wondering which of the consumer marketers he knows might be able to introduce him to the heads of the finance departments within their companies.

LOOKING FOR A JOB?
MAKE IT EASIER ON YOURSELF

Invariably, people—especially if they're on the far side of thirty-five—begin their job search (consciously or not) thinking they are entering into a permanently life-altering experience. Their reasoning sounds something like this: "I need to go into this search believing that my next job is going to be my last one, because I could be spending the rest of my working life at the place that hires me, so I have to make sure it's a perfect fit."

With that as the premise, we plan in painful detail—"I need to know exactly where within the subdivision's finance department I'll be working"—before we take action like sending out an email to a friend of a friend of a friend in the company that we *know*, after weeks of research, is the place we want to work.

Not only is this needlessly stressful—do you really want to agonize over every aspect of your job search?—it is silly.

Odds are this isn't going to be your last job. The economy is simply evolving too fast for you to think you are going to work at one place for several decades. (Just ask the people formerly employed by Oldsmobile, Polaroid, Washington Mutual, Pets.com, or ....)

People under age 35 don't think their current employer is going to be their last one. If you're older than that, you shouldn't either.

So plan on moving from gig to gig. Acknowledging that fact will reduce your stress significantly.

As for the search itself, here's our advice: Figure out the following two things:

1. What truly tugs at your heart? What is going to make you excited to get up and go to work in the morning? (This is a variation on the "desire" discussion we had earlier.)

2. What are you willing to pay—in both the figurative and literal sense—in order to obtain that kind of work? Will you move? Take the night shift? Willingly work weekends? How much money do you need to make? Will you take a smaller salary in exchange for a commission or piece of the action, or the potential to receive huge bonuses?

Armed with the answers to those questions, spend some time—and we are talking hours, not days—thinking about two different things:

1. The kind of places that offer this kind of work.

2. How you can get in front of someone who is in the position to hire you. (Who do you know that these people know, and what is it going to take to get their attention, if you need to approach them directly?)

After repositioning his skills, the researcher discovers that the feedback he receives is more encouraging. As a result of the additional education, and the repositioning of his past work, he gets several serious interviews and is finally hired as the second-in-command of the R&D department of a large soft-drinks company.

WHAT IF YOU ARE JUST STARTING OUT?

If you are entering the workforce for the first time, you are at the perfect point to use the Act. Learn. Build. Repeat. model. Your options are just about limitless and, since you have limited resources to begin with, you have virtually nothing to lose should whatever you try not work out.

Sarah Ashley Pavlik serves as a good example. She graduated law school in 2011, but put off taking the bar exam in order to join an Orange County, California, venture capital firm that focused on funding clean-technology companies. The firm became a victim of the Great Recession, and so Sarah is now once again trying to figure out what she wants to do with her working life.

She has several paths to choose from. She could, of course, "simply" become a lawyer and become entrepreneurial by starting her own practice, as opposed to joining an established firm. Indeed, she recently took the bar exam and is awaiting the results.

But while she could choose to be employed by someone else (by joining a law firm), Sarah has other options. One is to work on what we think is a great idea—a personal alarm clock that would awaken only you and not the person sleeping next to you. (We don't want to give away too many details, so we will leave it at that.) She could develop that idea on her own, or take the idea to an existing company and use it as a calling card to get a job.

The other option could take her down one of two different paths. But the starting point is the same in either case.

Once people learn that you've gone to law school, it's pretty common for them to ask you for (unpaid) legal advice. Sarah noticed that most of the questions she got came from women, particularly those who needed more than a yes or no answer. Some of them were "trapped with a bad prenup" or had been "suckered into a bad business deal"—and many just didn't know where to turn to get good legal advice.

Hearing the predicaments of these women suggested an opportunity to Sarah. Could she create a referral service—à la Angie's List, which provides recommendations for home repairs and healthcare— where someone could get the name of a well-qualified lawyer, accountant, financial planner, or whatever professional they needed—someone who would have been well vetted?

It seems like it is a market need waiting to be filled.

Sarah has a couple of options if she wants to pursue it. She can go the traditional route, raise a lot of money, hire folks to do research about what exactly is needed in the marketplace, and launch a full-blown marketing campaign announcing what she has.

Or she can employ the Act. Learn. Build. Repeat. model. She could start, for example, by engaging with one of the women needing help. Would that woman pay Sarah for finding her the right resource? Would lawyers, accountants, or other professionals pay what would be in essence a referral fee, if Sarah provided them clients? Taking small steps down that path could lead to all kinds of directions, including taking her idea to existing referral services and joining their idea with hers.

It will be interesting to see how it plays out.

REENTERING THE WORKFORCE

If you have been out of work for a while, for whatever reason, clearly you want to draw on all the points we made previously about how to get moving. But let us offer one more piece of advice.

In an interview where he tried to explain why he excelled as a hockey player, Wayne Gretzky famously said, "I skate to where the puck is going to be." You need to follow the same approach.

If you have been out of the workforce for a while, you will naturally be inclined to begin by building off where you left off. That is understandable, but wrong. The marketplace will have changed (perhaps radically) since you were last in it. You need to adjust to where it is going, not where it was. You want to take a look to see where you fit today, and what you need to do to fit better. That could mean you may have to take courses and/or reposition the way you present yourself. Or, as in the case of Sarah Ashley Pavlik, think about ways you can make what you want to do fit within an existing organization.

You could look at this as bad news—because it sounds like a lot of work—but it really isn't. By virtue of being out of the workforce for a while, you are less encumbered than others. You aren't locked into doing the same thing that you used to. You have the opportunity to go in a new direction.

WHAT WE JUST COVERED

1. It doesn't matter if you have been fired, are looking for your first job, or are reentering the workforce after being out of it for a while. The Act. Learn. Build. Repeat. model can be extremely helpful.

2. Instead of planning for the long term, concentrate on what you can do immediately that will get you as close as possible to what you want to be doing.

3. Remember, your next job is probably not your last. That understanding may eliminate some of the pressure associated with looking for a new job . . . or starting a business of your own.

CHAPTER 10

You Must Remember This:
Concluding Thoughts

"Life is what happens to you while you're busy making other plans."

—John Lennon

We began the book talking about how difficult it is to convince people that their jobs are in jeopardy. We're going to end the same way.

You know the odds say the swirling global economy is going to whisk you out of a job. Change does that. It always has. Heck, economist Joseph Schumpeter wrote about that fact seventy years ago when he coined the phrase "creative destruction" (in his book *Capitalism, Socialism, and Democracy*) to explain how economic forces are always disrupting the economy—and the people who work within it. Just about every day you can read a newspaper account or watch a broadcast that reinforces that Schumpeter was right.

But since "nothing is constant but change" was probably already a cliché when the Greek philosopher Heraclitus said it 2,700 years ago, we need to make the point another way. Try this:

Imagine it is twenty years ago. On a random Saturday morning, you slip on your American-made polo shirt and made-in-the-USA blue jeans, and while walking downtown to see your travel agent you wonder if that new CD you want—the one that has been sold out forever—is finally available. Spotting a pay phone, you get the number for a record store you know is nearby. Yes, they have a copy that they will put aside for you, if you can get there within the hour. Not quite certain where the store is, you go back to your car and pull out a map of downtown and double-check. You'll head right over after you pick up your plane tickets at the travel agency.

As you consider this scenario, and countless others you could imagine, you realize that it's easier to list the tiny handful of professions and industries that will remain unchanged in the *next* twenty years than it is to write down the ones that will likely be altered—radically. And that is why all that upheaval is likely to throw you—and anyone else who is not prepared—out of a job.

You say that's hyperbolic? Well, hopefully you have a different view now, after reading this book. But if you still have your doubts, consider this: Our guess is that the American textile workers who made those polo shirts and blue jeans, and the people who produced those CDs and sold them, and the long-time employees who manufactured pay phones and printed maps never thought markets and technologies would evolve as quickly as they did. Travel agents, we are sure, felt the same way.

They were in denial. And most of us are, too.

DOIN' WHAT *DOES NOT* COME NATUR'LLY

We've argued throughout that everyone will have to become entrepreneurial. And some people take to the idea of becoming an entrepreneur as if they were born to it. They absolutely love it. But do you have to feel that way?

Absolutely not.

You can use entrepreneurship as a means to whatever end you wish to accomplish. The ideas we have advocated will work just about anywhere.

The fact is, the rate of change is only increasing. And the only thing you are able to count on when it comes to how you are going to make your living, from today forward, is *you*. And that's why it's in your best interest to start mastering entrepreneurial thought and action, practicing the Act. Learn. Build. Repeat. model we have discussed throughout.

In the best of worlds (i.e., you get to keep your current, enjoyable job) you will gain new skills and new ways of thinking that will allow you to perform your work better. If all the economic turmoil upends your company, you can take that new learning and use it for someone else's benefit—by taking a new job, or becoming a consultant, or perhaps serving on a board.

And if the worst happens—the winds of change do indeed sweep you out the door—you will have a head start on whatever it is you do next, which could involve starting a business of your own.

The takeaway from any of these scenarios: No matter what happens in the economy, you need to be prepared to be entrepreneurial, if not actually being an entrepreneur.

WHAT HAVE WE LEARNED?

We talked to literally hundreds of entrepreneurs in researching this book. When people ask us what we have learned about entrepreneurs and the people who become entrepreneurs, here are the first three things that come to mind:

1. **They don't like risk.** There's a reason that seasoned entrepreneurs don't think of themselves as risk takers, even though everyone else does. They have developed terrific ways to limit potential losses as they start a new venture. While they don't like risk, they accept it as part of the game and then work extremely hard to reduce it to a minimum. (See the discussion in Chapter 4.) They don't bet the house because they know they are always going to need a place to live.

2. **They don't overthink.** If they are facing a situation they have seen before, or one where data is readily available, entrepreneurs rely on what has happened in the past. They use what has worked before. But when they are facing an unknown future—will their new

product or service be a success? Is their community going to accept the nonprofit idea they are passionate about?—they don't spend a lot of time thinking. When they can't predict the future, they act—which brings us to our third point.

3. **They act by taking a small (inexpensive) step toward their goal.** They pause to see what they learned from taking that step. And then, if it makes sense, they build off what they have learned and take another small step. They follow this Act. Learn. Build. Repeat. model until they either achieve what they want, decide it can't be done, or choose to do something else.

As we said throughout, the person who ultimately will decide your future is you. We have explained as clearly as we can what we think the economy is going to look like going forward, and what we think is the best way to navigate the uncertainty we all face.

It is up to you to determine what you want to do.

We wish you the best of luck.

APPENDIX A

Teaching the ALBR Model

The ALBR approach can also work in our schools—up to and including college. Instituting this model would be wonderful, since the earlier we learn entrepreneurial skills, the better off we all will be. Let's see how it could be done.

It would be lovely to think that you could easily introduce the ALBR approach to problem solving into your local school system. And while the reality is you *could*—it would just serve as an additional block of material that would be taught whenever the curriculum called for a discussion of how to deal with uncertainty—in social studies when you were discussing how public policy is created, for example—the reality is it is not that simple.

School systems are overwhelmed these days with demands coming at them from all sides. Attracting good teachers remains difficult, and the idea of adding "one more brick to the load," which is how administrators are likely to see a request to teach ALBR, is not going to be received well. Nonetheless, if you want to take a shot trying to convince your local school board that it's a good idea—and we hope that by now you have seen that it is—by all means try.

But let us give you a couple of alternatives to employ as well. We aren't going to go into this in endless depth. How to reform our nation's schools is not the primary purpose of this book. However, the following will give you a flavor of how this might work.

With that throat clearing out of the way, perhaps the most effective thing you could do is teach the ALBR method to your children yourself. The benefits are twofold:

1. Your kids will get more individual attention. No matter how great the school system your child attends, no one cares as much about their future as you do.

2. As the old saying goes, the best way to learn something is to teach it.

Will your kids be receptive? Probably. All the kids we know are frustrated with being told that "someday" they'll discover this subject (geometry, biology, English, whatever) will be interesting, useful, and relevant to their lives. If you could make it so, they would be more than willing to listen.

How might this play out? Here's one of our favorite examples. Eight-year-old Andrea is extremely bright: the world's biggest New York Mets fan, and someone who believes with all her heart that math is "stupid."

Not surprisingly, she finds fractions and decimals difficult.

A very enterprising parent turned Andrea from someone who hated doing arithmetic into a young lady who tells everyone she meets that she is going to be a math major in college and, when she graduates, she is going to be the next Bill James (the baseball statistics guru). And the process took all of twenty minutes.

How did this transformation take place? Her mom asked her a couple of simple questions while they were having breakfast one Monday morning.

Mom: *Andrea, I saw [Mets third baseman] David Wright went three for eight in yesterday's doubleheader. Do you know what he hit for the day?*

As you can see, Andrea's mother knew what her desire was: She wanted for her daughter to be interested in math. So she also took Action with a small step toward making her desire a reality by engaging with Andrea in a subject she knew her daughter loved—baseball.

Andrea: *.375.*

Mom: *That's right. Do you know how to figure that out?*

Andrea didn't. All she knew was the announcers said you were hitting .375 if you went three for eight. But now that her mother asked, she desperately wanted to know how to figure it out. That curiosity proved to Andrea's mother that the idea of using baseball for teaching her daughter math was right. The mom promptly went into the Learn part of the model.

Mom: *Well, if you set it up like a fraction, you would put the three in the numerator and the eight in the denominator. Like this.*

Mom shows her by writing out the equation:

$$\frac{3}{8}$$

Andrea realized her mother was reintroducing the subject of fractions, but for the first time, she thought there might be a worthwhile payoff, so she continued to pay attention as her mother talked.

> **Mom:** *And what we would do is divide the denominator into the numerator, or divide eight into three, and you would get .375. That's why all batting averages begin with a decimal.*

This explanation is the Build part of the model. For the first time ever, math was relevant to Andrea. And she instantly wanted to move on to the Repeat part.

> **Andrea:** *How would you figure out [pitcher] R. A. Dickey's earned run average? [Andrea remained a fan of Dickey's even though the Mets had traded her favorite pitcher to Toronto, of all places.]*

> **Mom:** *That's a little harder, but not much. It is just another example of what you have been studying in math class. The formula would look like this.*

Mom again writes the equation:

$$\frac{\text{Earned Runs}}{\text{Innings Pitched}} \times 9 = \text{ERA}$$

> **Mom:** *So if R. A. Dickey is charged with 22 earned runs in his first 99 innings pitched, his ERA would be 22 divided by 99, which is .2222, times 9, which works out to 1.99—a very good number.*

Andrea had been introduced to the Act. Learn. Build. Repeat. model. She was hooked.

The approach doesn't have to be this tailored, of course. Another way to introduce the ALBR model to children is to literally have them create a lemonade stand. That's what Babson College, together with the city of Boston, local businesses in the city, youth organizations, and a handful of philanthropists have done.

With the help of adult volunteers, young entrepreneurs learn how to establish a business (the lemonade stand) and all that comes with it—such as setting goals and creating and executing a detailed business plan. In short, by following the ALBR model, they learn the entrepreneurial skills necessary to be successful in the future and become contributing members of their communities.

"When we teach students entrepreneurship, we teach them to invent their future," stated then–Boston Mayor Thomas M. Menino. "Lemonade Day Boston is a wonderful, important way to help Boston's young people become part of our innovation economy."

You can learn more about this at Boston.LemonadeDay.org, where the slogan is "today lemonade, tomorrow the world." (And to see how the ALBR model could be applied to middle schools, see One Hen.org and the way it approaches teaching micro-finance.)

HOW THE ENTREPRENEURIAL MIND-SET IS CHANGING ONE BUSINESS SCHOOL: A CASE STUDY

The central idea of this book is that everyone will have to become an entrepreneur, or at the very least master entrepreneurial thought and action, to thrive in the workplace in the years ahead. It is encouraging to see that the message is getting through, at least to some extremely bright business school students.

Joe Haslam, an associate professor at IE Business School in Madrid, Spain, as well as the chairman of Hot Hotels, a same-day hotel reservation smartphone app, told us about three trends he sees with his students.

1. Instead of looking at jobs listings or going to a recruiting event, many students contact senior company executives (not HR!) directly. That's what Sophie, a French student, did, saying: "You should be doing X, Y, and Z—and your company should hire me to do it."

2. They are setting up a business designed not to make a profit, but to get the attention of a larger company where they want to work. It's easier to get a meeting with someone when you are a company founder instead of an MBA student. For example, Amit is an Israeli law graduate whose career objective is to be a general counsel for a large corporation. He figures the best way to get noticed is by working on a start-up. The company may come to nothing, but the real-world experience he will get, and the contacts he will make, will be much more useful to him than any MBA project.

3. They trade skills in the new economy for skills in the old. For example, Nour is a Moroccan entrepreneur with an ambitious idea for a social network based on trust between users. Her plan is to knock on doors of

boutique private equity houses and convince them to work with her for free. She'll get a professional plan and they get an enhanced understanding of the new start-up economy.

"In all the examples," Haslam says, "the students have used an entrepreneurial mind-set to get ahead." He—and they—are absolutely right.

APPENDIX B

Using ALBR in the Public Sector

It doesn't matter if we are talking about the federal government or the town council of Anna Maria, Florida (population 1,549). Everyone will agree that our current level of governance leaves a lot to be desired.*

It would seem the Act. Learn. Build. Repeat. model could be of service, if we are hoping for new approaches to improve things.

However, using the ALBR method when working with government brings the same sorts of challenges as applying it within your local school system. Budgets are tight. And the people in charge are, as a rule, not the most creative types. (In large part, that is not their

---

* A recent headline from Anna Maria's weekly paper makes the point: "Council rejects its own plan."

fault. Governing by consensus means—almost by definition—that radical departures from the norm are going to be rare.)

But all that said, it can be done. The approach and the principles work the same way we have discussed. Let's take the idea of creating a fictional community recreation center to show how this could work.

The national mood about spending the public's money being what it is, the odds of getting your local municipality to allocate $5 million to get a fully functioning facility built are extremely remote. So, what do you do?

Well, step one is to figure out if anyone other than you thinks the recreation center is a good idea. And by canvassing the town—and convincing the local weekly newspaper to conduct a poll—you discover that there is demand. In fact, too much demand. People responded that there's a need for an indoor pool, indoor skateboarding ramps, and a place to play basketball. Plus, there's a small but intense desire for a place to play hockey and ice skate, and for racquetball courts as well.

Given the response, you have confirmation that your idea is valid.

Armed with the data, you go back to town hall and the response is still no-go, but this time one of the selectmen makes an interesting offhand comment: "You know, Calvin Coolidge Elementary School has been vacant ever since we decided to combine it with Millard Fillmore K through 3 and have all the kids go there. I think the town council could be convinced to sell you the building for $1, and waive all the required permit fees, provided you had a way to fund the cost of retrofitting the structure."

The great news about that comment was that not only did you gain the town's (unofficial) endorsement, but you also probably shaved $1 million off the construction price. True, the elementary school would probably have to be gutted, but the shell could easily remain; you wouldn't have to buy the land, and the parking lot is already in place. The less-than-good news? You haven't a clue about where you are going to get the "remaining" $4 million.

What's the next step? If you think back to Chapter 4, you'll remember that two of the pivotal questions to always ask when you are trying to start something new are:

1. What resources can I draw on? and

2. Who can I bring along to help make my idea a reality?

In this case, the answers overlap. The biggest resource you can draw on is your address book, which contains the phone numbers of most of the town's unofficial leaders. You invite everyone over to your house for coffee and a discussion about the recreation center. It quickly becomes clear that it is impossible to create one building that will accommodate everyone's needs at a reasonable cost. (There is simply no inexpensive way to put a heated swimming pool near an ice rink.) But if you can eliminate either the pool or the rink, everything else could work within one building.

The group takes an informal vote and the decision is that the swimming pool was more desirable than the skating rink. (The folks who really wanted a place to play hockey and figure skate were understandably disappointed, but said they would look into getting a building of their own.)

With the idea of a recreation complex that would have a pool, basketball and racquetball courts, and a place to skateboard agreed upon, the question is how to make it a reality.

Not surprisingly, the people in our example used the ALBR model to figure out what to do next.

One of the major building blocks of the ALBR model is understanding current reality to know exactly where you stand. So, the group went to a local architect, one who volunteered his services, to come up with a firm estimate of how much money they would actually need to retrofit the building.

"It comes to $3.8 million," the architect said as he presented drawings of what the complex could look like. "About two-thirds of that is going to be labor."

That sparked an idea. Clearly, there would be specialized skills they would have to hire—indoor demolition can be tricky—but couldn't they do a lot of work themselves? One of the biggest contractors in the state lived in town. They approached him and he "volunteered" one of his senior people to do a breakdown on what would need to be done by professionals and what could be handled by volunteers. (The woman would also serve—at no cost—as the general contractor for the project should the group decide to go ahead.) Her estimate: Of the $2.5 million labor costs (two-thirds of the $3.8 million construction budget), about $1.5 million could be handled by volunteers.

That left $1 million for specialized labor and another $1 million in materials. Yes, $2 million was a daunting number. But it was far better than $3.8 million and 60 percent less than what everyone thought the project was going to cost when they began. And they were able to whittle that cost down further. A quick check with local building products suppliers showed that they would be willing to provide the necessary lumber, plumbing, fixtures, and the like at cost in exchange for discrete advertising within the complex. That saved another $500,000.

The group set off to figure out how to raise $1.5 million and coordinate the volunteers.

GETTING TO THE RIBBON-CUTTING CEREMONY

The fund-raising itself was relatively simple. The community did what it always did when there was a project to be funded that the town council wouldn't support. It just did it in a far bigger way.

In addition to the car washes and bake sales, folks got creative. They sold naming rights to the center for $75,000. (An anonymous donor asked that it be named after a local boy who died fighting in Afghanistan.) The naming rights for the basketball courts, racquetball courts, and skateboarding ramps went for an additional $25,000 each. Raffles for a new car are not uncommon in community fundraising, but in this case two new Lamborghinis were auctioned off. (The dealer donated them at cost, and by the time the bidding was done, the community had another $500,000.) And so it went until all the money was raised.

We are happy to tell you that the Lt. Thomas Michael Smith Recreation Center is now functioning seven days a week, 363 days a year (closing only on Thanksgiving and Christmas Day). The story of how this facility came into being shows that the Act. Learn. Build. Repeat. model can work in nonprofit settings as well.

INDEX